D0535182

VEGETABLES

The American Horticultural Society
Illustrated Encyclopedia of Gardening

VEGETABLES

The American Horticultural Society
Mount Vernon, Virginia

For The American Horticultural Society

President
Dr. Gilbert S. Daniels

Technical Advisory Committee
Dr. Henry M. Cathey
Everett Conklin
Mary Stuart Maury

Vegetables Staff for The Franklin Library/Ortho Books

Editorial Director
Min S. Yee

Supervisory Editor
Lewis P. Lewis

Editor
A. Cort Sinnes

Art Director
John A. Williams

Creative Director
Michael Mendelsohn

Contributing Writers
Walter L. Doty
Lance Walheim

Contributing Photographers
Clyde Childress
William Aplin
Michael Landis
Lee Blodget
All-America Selections staff
W. Atlee Burpee Co. staff
George W. Park Seed Co. staff

Illustrator
Ron Hildebrand

Production Director
Robert Laffler

Production Manager
Renee Guilmette

For Ortho Books

Publisher
Robert L. Iacopi

For The Franklin Library

Publisher
Joseph Sloves

The cover photograph shows a collection of fresh vegetables from the garden—from top to bottom, crookneck squash, yellow straightneck squash, squash, cucumber, tomatoes, red pepper, turnip, scallop or pattypan squash, butternut squash, pumpkin, carrots, scallions, and zucchini. Photograph by Robert Brandau.

Consultants (vegetable specialists and researchers):

Earl J. Allen
University of Arkansas
James R. Baggett
Oregon State
Kermit Hildahl
Iowa State
John MacGillivray
University of California
Bernard L. Pollack
Rutgers State University, New Jersey
Wayne Sitterly
Agricultural Experiment Station,
Clemson University, South Carolina
E. Blair Adams
University of Wyoming
Albert A. Banadyga
North Carolina State University
Richard L. Bernard
U.S. Regional Soybean Laboratory, Illinois
Louis Berninger
University of Wisconsin
James T. Garrett
Mississippi State University
A. E. Griffiths
University of Rhode Island
Herbert Hopen
University of Illinois
Anton S. Horn
University of Idaho
N. S. Mansour
Oregon State
Dean Martin
South Dakota State
Charles W. Marr
Kansas State
Charles A. McClurg
University of Maryland
R. R. Rothenberger
University of Missouri
Donald Schuder
Purdue University, Indiana
Raymond Sheldrake
Cornell University, New York
W. L. Sims
University of California
Perry M. Smith
Auburn University, Alabama
Cecil L. Thomson
University of Massachusetts
James Utzinger
Ohio State
Ben Vance
Iowa State
George R. Williams
Virginia Polytechnic Institute

Special Consultants:

Maggie Baylis
Russell Beatty
University of California
J. D. Carlisle
J. R. Cheatham
George Creed
George Dewey
Andrew A. Duncan
University of Minnesota
W. A. Frazier
Oregon State
Fred Peterson
Victor Pinckney Jr.
William Titus
Doris Tuinstra
Walter Vodden
Blake Garden, Kensington, California
Frits Went
Desert Research Institute, University of Nevada
Jack Chandler
Richard Westcott
John Matthias
John M. Bridgman
Aaron Keiss

Produced under the authorization of The American Horticultural Society by The Franklin Library and Ortho Books.

Copyright © 1974, 1976, 1980 by Ortho Books
Special contents © 1980 by The American Horticultural Society. All rights reserved under International and Pan-American Copyright Conventions.

Every effort has been made at the time of publication to guarantee the accuracy of the names and addresses of information sources and suppliers and in the technical data contained. However, the subscriber should check for his own assurance and must be responsible for selection and use of suppliers and supplies, plant materials and chemical products.

No portion of this book may be reproduced in any form or by any means without permission first being requested and obtained from The American Horticultural Society, c/o The Franklin Library, Franklin Center, Pennsylvania, 19091. Portions of this volume previously appeared in the Ortho Books *All About Vegetables, Gardening Shortcuts, Weather-Wise Gardening,* and *Fundamentals of Gardening.*

Library of Congress Catalog Card Number 80-80416

Printed in the United States of America.

12 11 10 9

A Special Message from
The American Horticultural Society

This volume in *The Illustrated Encyclopedia of Gardening* stands, we believe, as the clearest and most practical guide to vegetable gardening we know of. It is a book about the whole gardening process—not simply a book on how to grow vegetables. Nor is it a paean to the vegetable. There are many books like that. Rather, it contains a wealth of knowledge, lore, advice, tips, cautions, information, and common sense about growing vegetables successfully and pleasurably.

There are straightforward, no-nonsense procedures for the beginning gardener as well as experienced advice and encouragement for the seasoned gardener. The illustrations, charts, and diagrams show *exactly* how to do what the text describes. We try to ensure that no step is overlooked.

People have been growing vegetables for millenia. The original purpose was the need for food—and of course home gardens are still a major source of food for millions of people today. But for many other more fortunate millions it is the preference for good, fresh vegetables at a reasonable cost that turns them into vegetable gardeners. They may not have to garden, but they want to.

Vegetables is really for them. Any kind of gardening requires a certain amount of work and, above all, regular attention. But this book makes it as easy and uncomplicated as possible. It should be a satisfying pleasure, not a chore. Too many would-be gardeners have become prematurely discouraged and have given up because their first enthusiastic efforts have gradually turned into unwelcome drudgery. This is the pity—because no garden should be a burden. With sensible planning and a realistic evaluation of the time and space that can be devoted to a garden, anyone should be able to cultivate vegetables comfortably and rewardingly.

It is the planning that transforms a grower into a gardener, and *Vegetables* should help you to become a first-rate gardener. With pleasure.

Gilbert S. Daniels
President

CONTENTS

Introduction   10

You can use this book in a variety of ways, whether you are an expert, a gardener with a couple of seasons' experience behind you, or a beginner. This chapter describes how each level of gardener can best use the material in this volume. It also offers some unconventional advice about the right approach to take to the specifics of vegetable growing.

Climate and Gardening   16

Although each vegetable has its own set climate requirements, there is considerable latitude among those requirements, and you can do much to modify your own climate for the benefit of the plant. This chapter offers advice on mulching, wind and frost protection, assessing the "little climates" around your yard, with maps and descriptions of the growing regions of the U.S.

The Basics of Vegetable Gardening

A working knowledge of the important basics—soil, water, and fertilizers—is the cornerstone for all good garden practices. This chapter tells you what you need to know relative to growing vegetables. Also included is information on artificial soil mixes, the important relationship between soil type and watering methods, composting instruction, and how to read a fertilizer label.

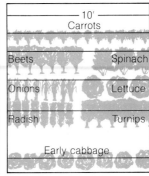

Planning the Garden

Every successful vegetable garden starts with a plan on paper; it's the only way to ensure that the produce that comes out of the garden corresponds to the needs of the people who planted it. Although planning is an essential step, it's also a fun step, allowing you time for book-reading, catalog browsing, and little day dreaming. This chapter shows how to estimate harvests properly and plan for a succession of them.

Planting and Care

Now that it's time to actually plant, you must decide whether to put seed directly in the soil or start it indoors; how and when to bring transplants outdoors; whether to use a plastic mulch to hurry the season; and how deep and how far apart in the row to plant seed. This chapter covers these questions and more, including pest and disease control, advice on rotation, and using disease-resistant varieties.

Small Space Gardening

Gardeners with limited amounts of space have come up with ingenious methods of solving the problem. The raised bed filled with artificial soil mix has been very successful, as have vegetables in containers, vertical growing areas and hanging baskets. This chapter explores these and other small-space gardening ideas.

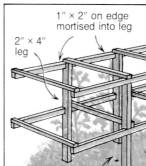

1" × 2" on edge
mortised into leg

2" × 4"
leg

Experienced Advice

If you don't have a good neighbor, who's full of over-the-back-fence gardening advice, or if your neighbor knows no more about gardening than you do, this chapter will especially interest you. It contains good ideas from gardeners all over the country, and discusses everything from gopher protection to vegetable washing.

Encyclopedia of Vegetables

What do you want to know about a vegetable? Its historical background; cultural advice; what varieties perform best in your area; mistakes beginners make; problems you are likely to encounter; how to harvest the crop? All the information you need is in this comprehensive chapter, from artichokes to zucchini.

VEGETABLES

For many gardeners, young and old alike, a
vegetable garden in its full glory is the highlight
of the summer season.

INTRODUCTION

*This chapter tells you how to use
this book and how to make the
most of the information in it for
successful and uncomplicated
vegetable gardening.*

Vegetable growing doesn't have to be a complicated business, nor do we have
any intention of making it so. In fact, you could probably put this book aside
and proceed perfectly adequately on your own. That may seem a strange thing
to say in a book about vegetable gardening, but stop for a moment and think
what you would do. Very likely you would go to your local garden center and
buy some seeds, some fertilizer, some manure, and a bale or two of peat moss.
Then you would spade up the soil in the sunniest spot you could find, spread
the peat moss and manure over the soil, and add the fertilizer to that, according
to the directions on the package. You would work the manure, peat and fertilizer into the soil with a cultivator, rake, or rented tiller. Then you would read
the directions on the seed package to find out about planting seeds, thinning,
and distance between rows. And finally you would plant the seeds. Millions
of gardeners have raised billions of pounds of beautiful vegetables in just this
way, by trial and error aided by common sense.

But if you do want some useful ideas and suggestions, we hope you will use
this book. It will help you avoid some errors and add a little excitement and a lot
of knowledge to your gardening experience.

The Basic Facts

If you prefer to skip the rest for now and get right down to the basic how-to-
plant information, turn to the planting chart on pages 56 and 57. You may
need to consult it when you plan your garden, as well as when you plant it.

But the information in the chart isn't just about *how* to plant. The three
columns headed "Needs cool soil," "Tolerates cool soil," and "Needs warm soil"
offer good clues on *when* to plant. For more specific advice see the "When to
plant" section for each major vegetable. At lease, this will keep you from planting peas and beans on the same day.

Watch for the cautionary headings, "Mistakes beginners make," that appear
throughout the book. These will help you avoid potential hazards.

About The Plants You Can't Grow

If plants you can't grow—or you think you can't grow—are discussed in your
climate, don't take it to heart. There are too many gardeners who manage to
grow what "can't be grown"—and enjoyably, too. If you want to grow a particular plant strongly enough, you'll grow it—even if you have to build a special
climate around it.

Putting First Things First

No matter how much you improve your soil, or how expertly you plant your
seed, or how conscientiously you fertilize, all may be lost if you omit one step:
weeding. In the competition between weeds and newly emerged seedlings, a
few days of neglect on your part will give the weeds a definite edge.

However, you can learn to enjoy hand weeding. When you kneel, squat, or

sit, you are looking at your plants from eye level. When you pull a grassy weed that is about to strangle a carrot seedling, you can view it as an act of kindness that surely will be rewarded. If the tops of the weeds break off, you know that the soil is too dry. This proves how quickly weeds can rob your seedlings of water and nutrients.

How To Avoid Disappointments

Some of the gardeners we worked with share their successes and disappointments in "The Spoilers" on page 59, and their discoveries in "Experienced Advice" on pages 68-73. These gardening confessions may help you. And pay attention to the "Mistakes beginners make" entries, and use them to point you toward success, rather than to warn you of disaster.

Most of our gardening friends and workers felt that their successes outweighed their disappointments. In answer to the question, "Did anything surprise you?" one gardener replied, "How well things grow under the right conditions, and how poorly under the wrong conditions."

Planning The Garden

There is a world of difference between *growing vegetables* and *vegetable gardening*.

Vegetable gardening calls to mind a particular sequence of questions: What should you grow in the space you have? What varieties? When should you start? When is the first harvest? How can you stretch the harvest with a succession of plantings? Vegetable gardening is a mind-bending exercise in juggling space and time. (But you'll find help in planning gardens, from box sizes to 25- by 30-footers, on pages 42-47.)

Growing vegetables, on the other hand, can be accomplished without a conventional vegetable garden and without growing huge quantities of vegetables. Vegetables can grow in a flower border and in boxes and tubs.

Looking For The Hard-To-Find

Each year, more unusual "vegetables" are made available to seed companies. If a newly introduced vegetable is in the hard-to-find class, you'll find its catalog number or numbers in this book following the item. This number is keyed to

Even the common vegetable varieties grown in the home garden come from diverse climatic backgrounds: **1.** peppers from the Caribbean, **2.** lettuce from the Mediterranean, **3.** the eggplant from India, **4.** the tomato from South America, **5.** the cucumber from India, **6.** the carrot from the Mediterranean...

the number of a seed company, listed on page 140, that can supply you with that vegetable.

If the items are carried by a number of the seed companies, we did not key them because you can find these in four or more of the catalogs from the seed companies on the list.

Plus or Minus

We give what appear to be precise measurements in pounds, square feet, and length of row for applying fertilizers, as well as dates or charts for planting times. Seed-planting directions are expressed in inches between plants and between rows, and sometimes in degrees of temperature.

A glance at these measurements might lead you to believe that there is an exact formula for the care and feeding of each vegetable. But there are no precise recipes for growing plants. The situation more closely resembles using an oven with unknown temperature controls, flour that varies from fine to coarse, milk that may be sweet or sour, and water of unknown quality. Despite all the unknown factors, however, you still can grow perfect vegetables. This proves that the measurements are not critical. There's plenty of room for error.

You can use the dates, pounds, and inches mainly as reference points, making the adjustments necessary to manage your own climate and particular piece of soil. But you can only get the experience that allows you to make those adjustments by actually growing the plants.

Many gardeners measure fertilizer by the handful or by how it looks scattered on the soil, and let the plants' color, size of leaf, or rate of growth signal them when to apply it. But the problem with measuring by instinct is that when you get exceptional results, you have no way of duplicating the treatment. And the problem with letting the plant tell you when to fertilize is that by then it may be too late to do any good.

...**7.** the kohlrabi from Northern Europe, **8.** the cabbage from Central Europe, and **9.** beans from Central America.

Challenge The Authorities

Don't blindly accept the recipes and directions in this book or any other. Only the plants in your garden can tell you the truth—and the plant is always right, no matter what an authority has said. Dr. Frits Went, a noted scientist and horticulturist, says it this way:

"Once the amateur has realized that he himself is master of the situation in his garden, and that he is not the slave of a set of recipes, a great deal is gained. Gardening comes out of the realm of mystic beliefs and becomes an adventure in adaptation. Each plant grown becomes an experiment, instead of a routine performance. That plant becomes the test whether the applied principle was right. If the plant does not grow well or dies, the application of the principles was not right, or the conditions were such that the principle did not work. If, on the other hand, the plant behaves well, it shows the applicability of the principle.

"By looking at the plants in this way, a garden becomes immensely interesting, it becomes the testing ground of ideas, and it frees the mind from dogmatism. The gardener becomes aware of the fact that experiments can be carried out everywhere, and are not restricted to highly specialized laboratories.

"Science is not a cult; it flourishes where these observations are faithfully recorded."

Rows and Bands

In the planting chart and in the planting directions for the individual vegetables, we spell out the space between plants in a row and the distance between rows.

If you are a first-time gardener who is anxious to make a small plot of ground produce a bumper crop, you may think that the distances between rows are unnecessarily wide. You can cheat on these distances, but this will make weeding and harvesting more difficult. And when you narrow the space between rows, you also narrow the space for the roots to run down in, so you

Right: The early spring vegetable garden shows a succession of lettuce plantings, interspersed with daffodils, calendula, and Swiss chard. Below: Close spacing, a fast succession of crops, and soil storage of root crops through the winter makes this plot of land extremely productive.

As anyone with a garden will tell you, homegrown vegetables aren't necessarily better than the store-bought variety—they just taste that way. A full basket during the fall harvest means a full pantry for the rest of the year.

have to compensate by fertilizing and watering more often. Crowding also cuts down on air circulation and invites foliage diseases.

It makes good sense to use a small piece of ground for a mass planting of vegetables.

For example, you can grow carrots or lettuce in the same way you would start a lawn. Sow the carrot seed as you would grass seed, and rake it in lightly. Cover with a thin mulch of ground bark, peat moss, or vermiculite, and water as you would a new lawn. The seeds will sprout in about the same time as a quality bluegrass would. A lawn of lettuce or carrots needs an initial overall thinning and then selective thinning, as you harvest them.

Fair Is Fair

It's a well-advertised belief that home-grown vegetables are superior to store-bought ones, which lose their fresh sunshine quality quickly after picking. After all, vegetables that must be picked green to allow for time in shipment lack the taste quality you'd expect of home-grown tomatoes and melons.

But home-grown quality does not come automatically. A first-time gardener can grow a tough, stringy beet or a bitter bunch of lettuce; and home-grown turnips and kohlrabi can be almost inedible if not harvested at the young, half-grown stage.

There is no need to downgrade commercially grown vegetables in order to elevate the home-grown varieties. Only when you grow the best varieties, give them the water and fertilizers they need, and harvest them at the right time will you have a taste worth bragging about: "So much better than that store-bought stuff."

Getting Along With Nature

On pages 16-33, you'll find suggestions on how to avoid losing battles with nature, how to alter unfavorable environments, and how to live with nature's whims and tricks. To be a natural gardener, you must swing with nature's rhythm.

A successful gardener should probably
become familiar with weather patterns
in the area and the telltale signs of clouds,
winds and temperature. But the weather you
can really influence is "the little climate"
immediately around your garden.

CLIMATE AND GARDENING

A gardener's advice is simple when it comes to dealing with nature: you strengthen your chances for success when you work with nature rather than against it.

Each vegetable has its own set of requirements for day length, day and night temperatures, light intensities, and heat units, and these requirements change during the various stages of growth of the vegetables.

At first, it might seem an awesome challenge to change your natural climate in order to protect or further the growth of vegetables, but it is one of the most rewarding gardening exercises you can do. And the resourcefulness of gardeners is astounding—see page 68 for proof.

How can you raise the temperature? Planting warm-season crops just south of a tall reflective surface such as a fence, a wall, or a row of corn or sunflowers, will create some additional warmth. Planting on a south-facing slope also will increase heat for young plants.

You can use plastic cottage-cheese containers and other such containers from the market, or plastic jugs with the bottom removed, for early protection of seedlings. One-gallon plastic milk bottles with the bottom removed and the cap left off make wonderful hot caps. Polyethylene plastic film, both clear and black, will change the temperature efficiently. Using this film as a mulch will work miracles with some vegetables.

Mulching

Mulching is perhaps the most rewarding action you can take in your vegetable garden. Even the sound of the word seems to soften up the soil.

You can use organic material, such as leaves, peat moss, straw, manure, sawdust, ground bark, compost and the like; or manufactured materials, such as polyethylene film, aluminum foil, or paper.

When you use the best of both materials, you join company not only with the ancients but also with today's agricultural technologists.

Bear in mind that in discussing the value of organic mulches in the vegetable garden, it is *summer* mulching that we are talking about.

Applying an organic mulch in early spring will slow down the soil's natural tendency to warm up as spring advances. And since an organic mulch acts as an insulating blanket that reduces solar radiation into the soil, it increases the chance of frost hazards.

Summer mulching vs. cultivation. If, after it has rained or you have watered by sprinkler irrigation, you find yourself going over the soil with a cultivator to break up surface crust, you need a mulch. Raindrops cement the soil by packing the small particles between the larger ones, thus plugging the pores and keeping water and rain from entering. A mulch breaks the pressure of the water drops and keeps pore spaces open.

Weed control. To control weeds, your organic mulch must be thick enough to keep weed seedlings from going through it on their own stored food. Perennial weeds will thrive in spite of organic mulches—or perhaps because of them. However, black plastic will take care of all kinds of weeds and grasses.

Above right: A mulch of ground bark cools the soil in this strawberry patch. Soil temperature extremes can be damaging to many plants. Above: Straw is a satisfactory mulch.

Experimental work has led to some interesting discoveries. The squash plant, above, is being grown on a sky blue plastic mulch that reportedly repels some insects.

Conserves moisture. Mulches slow down the evaporation of water from the upper 6 to 8 inches of soil. Tests show that merely shading the bare soil will reduce evaporation as much as 30 percent; but applying a straw mulch will reduce evaporation as much as 70 percent.

A mulch not only saves on water but also helps maintain a more even moisture supply.

Adds to plant root system. By insulating the top few inches of the soil from the sun's heat and maintaining soil moisture to the surface of the soil, a mulch gives the roots free run within the richest layers of the soil. Tests show that plant roots under the mulch develop as extensive a root system as they do under bare soil; and the surface roots are an added bonus.

Of course, if the lower layers of the soil are composed of materials such as slow-draining, tight clay that don't encourage full root development, the plant will concentrate most of its roots near the surface.

Less danger of rot. A mulch beneath unstaked tomatoes, summer squash, and cucumbers lessens the loss of fruit through rot. A tomato sitting on damp soil invites bacterial damage. Muddy splashes of rain may start rot in lettuce.

How thick should the mulch be? For fine materials such as sawdust, apply organic mulches 1 to 2 inches thick. For coarse materials such as straw, apply the mulches to around 4 inches thick.

The Pluses and Minuses of Mulching

Mulch	Chance in soil temperature	Performance
CLEAR PLASTIC	+10	Short rays of sun penetrate clear plastic and warm soil; plastic traps evaporating water. Increases early growth in cool season, also stimulates weed growth beneath plastic.
BLACK PLASTIC	+6	Short rays heat black plastic which in turn warm soil. Solves weed problem. Increases crop yields of many crops. Protects fruit of vine crops from rot. See text.
BROWN PAPER MULCH	as much as −8	Light brown paper mulch with thin plastic coating reflects most of the short rays from the sun. It's biodegradable. Soil temperatures are as much as 8° cooler than first inches of exposed soil. No weeds.
ALUMINUM COATED PLASTIC & FOIL	as much as −10	Reflective surface bounces back short rays from the sun. Soil temperatures are as much as 10° cooler than top inches of exposed soil. Research findings show that reflective surfaces repel aphids.
ORGANIC MULCHES	as much as −10	Thick mulch of organic matter stops sun's rays before they hit the soil. Soil surface layer as much as 10 degrees cooler than exposed soil. Stops most annual weeds if applied thick enough. Needs yearly additions.

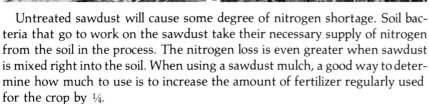

Untreated sawdust will cause some degree of nitrogen shortage. Soil bacteria that go to work on the sawdust take their necessary supply of nitrogen from the soil in the process. The nitrogen loss is even greater when sawdust is mixed right into the soil. When using a sawdust mulch, a good way to determine how much to use is to increase the amount of fertilizer regularly used for the crop by ¼.

Black plastic film. Black polyethylene has a solid reputation for increasing yields and speeding up ripening of melons, eggplant, peppers, and summer squash. In areas where early season temperatures are less than ideal for these warm-weather crops, this film has increased the yield of muskmelons in experimental plots up to 4 times that of nonmulched plants.

It is the increase in soil temperature that speeds up the growth so remarkably. Generally, however, this increase is only in the 3- to 6-degree range; sometimes it is only 2 degrees.

On a warm sunny day the temperature of the film soars, but reflects back to the air above it rather than transferring it to the soil.

Black polyethylene is generally available in 1 to 1½ mils thickness, in rolls 3 to 4 feet wide. Get the 1½-mil thickness. The usual method of spreading the film is illustrated on page 50.

In one of our test gardens, we spread the plastic wall to wall over the entire 20- by 30-foot plot. Since we had fought a losing battle with Bermuda grass the previous season, we figured the plastic was worthwhile as weed and grass control alone. We cut holes in the plastic and sowed seeds of melon and corn, according to our planting plan.

"Early" Varieties And Temperatures

If you live in a short-season climate, you can grow vegetables that normally require a long, warm growing season by planting "early" varieties.

In listing the varieties of vegetables, we indicated the number of days from seeding or transplanting to maturity after the name of the variety.

If you grow both "early" and "late" varieties you'll find the date valuable; but if you live in a cool-summer or short-season area, you'll find the date invaluable.

In such a case, the word "early" really means more than early: it means that the vegetable will grow and produce a crop with less total summer heat than the later-maturing varieties require.

The development of the "early" variety of the crenshaw melon expanded the plantings of this famous melon into relatively short-season areas.

The "midget" vegetables varieties, enthusiastically advertised as space savers for the mini-garden, are extra-early varieties, bred to grow with less total heat than other varieties. You can avoid frustration in growing vegetables if you accept the natural rhythm of plant growth rather than trying to make plants fit your rhythm. Spring fever in the first warm days of the season is not the best guide for when to plant. The full enjoyment of the vegetable garden comes when you are in step with beets, lettuce, beans, and all the vegetables you grow.

Check the planting chart on page 56-57. Are the vegetables you are thinking

1. The basic drawback of plastic mulches is that they must be removed at the end of the season, although, **2.** the future promises to bring degradable plastic mulches which will deteriorate after a specified time, and which can be incorporated into the soil.
3. These pumpkins were grown using a black plastic mulch. The mulch increased the soil temperature sufficiently to ripen the crop in a marginal growing climate, and reduced the incidence of rotting pumpkins.

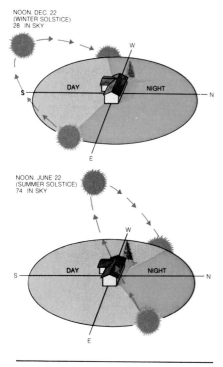

NOON, DEC. 22
(WINTER SOLSTICE)
28 IN SKY

NOON, JUNE 22
(SUMMER SOLSTICE)
74 IN SKY

of planting in the cool-season or warm-season group? If the former, you'll need a bit of discipline—you may have to plant some of the cool-weather crops before you quite *feel* like gardening.

"Cool-season" means more than that the vegetable can be planted early. It means that the temperature in which vegetables ripen determines their quality and good taste. With peas and beets, for example, the first harvest is the great one.

On the first warm day of spring, it may seem like nonsense to wait for the soil to warm up before planting beans and corn, or for the night temperatures to rise before setting out transplants of tomatoes—but if the soil temperature is below 55°, your beans will rot and your tomatoes and eggplants will just sit and sulk. Lima bean seed is likely to rot if the soil is below 62°; also okra.

Day Length

The length of day influences the growth habit of several annual vegetables. Spinach and Chinese cabbage are notorious examples. As days lengthen beyond the 12-hour day and 12-hour night of the vernal equinox (March 21), these vegetables get a signal that it's time to flower. Rising temperatures also play a part in this flowering habit. When your crops "bolt" to seed before they are ready to be harvested, you learn about the influence of day length first-hand.

If you have tried to grow Chinese cabbage in the spring, you know that it rates among the difficult-to-grow vegetables. But when grown to mature in the short days of fall, Chinese cabbage is as easy to grow as any other vegetable.

With spinach, long days cause bolting, especially if the plants were subjected to cool conditions when they were younger. To avoid this condition, use a "long-standing" variety and plant in early spring; or, in mild-winter climates, plant in fall.

Premature flowering also occurs in lettuce, but this is due more to hot weather than to day length. Choose varieties to fit the season. Check the variety list for bolt-resistant varieties.

Heat Units

Each vegetable has its own range of temperatures for maximum growth. Within this range, each has a minimum temperature below which it will not grow. The minimum for peas is 40°; for corn, 50°. Peppers and eggplant will live at 60°, but the optimum for growth is much higher. These warm-season plants have poor fruit size and quality at low temperatures.

This gardener has made the most of a narrow growing area next to a barn-red fence. The dark pigment of the fence absorbs the heat from the sun and radiates it back for the benefit of heat-loving vegetables and annuals.

The temperature requirements of warm-season vegetables are sometimes expressed in "heat-units." Gardeners have used heat units as one indication of which corn variety to select, although many other factors also are involved. However, comparing the heat units required for varieties of corn with the heat units provided by various climates shows why "early" varieties of corn are the best bets for cool or short-season areas.

Shade

You can't put a vegetable garden in a small area that has a tree or two if you believe what gardeners have been told since the first garden book was written —namely: "Locate the vegetable garden where it will get full sun."

But gardeners have been quite successful in growing many kinds of leafy vegetables in partial shade. *Minigardens for Vegetables,* the U.S.D.A. House and Garden Bulletin No. 163, provides an official sanction for planting in partial shade. The vegetables that tolerate partial shade are: beets, cabbage, carrots, chives, kale, leeks, lettuce, mustard, green onions, parsley, radishes, Swiss chard, and turnips.

All these vegetables are in the cool-season class. The warm-season crops, such as peppers, eggplant, and melons, require full sunlight.

Our consultant, A. E. Griffith of the University of Rhode Island, suggests that all advice about "part shade" should be qualified. Partial shade is one thing in a climate with a full quota of clear sunny days, and something else again in a climate where a cloud cover or fog reduces sunlight. "My reference to 'part shade' relative to cloud cover," he explains, "reflects a somewhat parochial thinking on my part.

"*Item:* Most vegetables do best in full sun in the cool, stormy summer climate of New England.

"*Item:* Most vegetables will tolerate shade for 2 to 3 hours per day, although they will not perform quite as well as they should.

"*Item:* Much of the coast of New England from eastern Connecticut eastward to New Brunswick is subject to fog or cloud overcast in May and June, as well as September and October, resulting in only about 65 percent of available sunshine.

"*Item:* Low solar energy plus partial shading would often seriously delay the maturation of many warm-weather crops."

Vegetable-Growing Climates

The maps on the following pages have been broken into three broad areas: the northern tier, the southern/central, and the western states. Different colored areas on the maps indicate the pattern in the last- and first-frost dates and the length of the growing season in 22 zones. You will find these zones referred to in the *When to Plant* information for the individual vegetables in the encyclopedia section.

Considering that the frost dates are the "normal" or "mean" dates, the chances of the frost hitting that date are exactly 50 percent. If you are a gambling gardener, you would do well to bet that the last frost of spring will be earlier and the first frost of fall or winter will be later.

Within each zone, the length of the growing season will vary as much as 20 days, due to differences in elevation, air drainage, and many other factors.

Even though the zones are not 100 percent accurate, it's worthwhile to locate yourself in your zone and to use the "When-to-plant" charts as a reference point for your own garden.

Look at the planting dates in your zone relative to the planting pattern of that vegetable in all the other zones. You can see at a glance the nature of the vegetable's adaptability.

Garden climates vary not just by the mile but by even a few feet. For instance, even a gentle slope in your garden has its effect, as the following quotation from Robert Moore Fisher's book, *How About the Weather,* illustrates.

Trellis training is an easy way to expand the growing season by placing the trellis in a section of the garden where there is more light and heat.

"Suppose, for instance, your home is located in Ohio. If the back yard is level, on a clear day at noontime in late winter it will receive an amount of sunshine normal for that date. If, however, your back yard slopes moderately toward the *north* at an angle of 1 foot in 12, it will receive a less-than-normal amount of sunshine. In fact, it will face the sun in about the same way that a level plot does in Ontario, Canada. Consequently, the 'private climate' of your sloping back yard will be as wintry as the 'private climate' of a level back yard in Ontario.

"On the other hand, should your back yard slope *southward* at an angle 1 foot in 12, it will receive more sunshine than normal. In this case, your back yard 'private climate' will be similar to the 'private climate' of a level back yard in warm, springlike South Carolina.

"The slope of land, therefore, influences the 'private climate' of back yards as much as latitude influences the 'public climate' of entire states." Only by living in a garden for years and keeping some kind of record of the yearly swing of temperatures can you learn to grow each vegetable in its most favorable time slot for your own area.

Beating the averages—planting earlier or later than a sensible person should —has its rewards. One freak early freeze may cut short the late-planted beans and corn 1 year out of 3, but out-of-season vegetables in the other years may make up for that failure.

The little climates. You can't do much about the big overall climate, but you can do a lot with the microclimates in your garden. You can make a warm area warmer by a windbreak; bring in more sunlight by thinning out overgrown trees; or lengthen the growing season by planting in raised beds, using a soil that drains quickly and warms up early in spring.

If you're a mini-gardener, you can enjoy a much longer growing season than if you're a dirt gardener. You don't have to wait for the soil to dry; at night you can just move the pots and boxes to protect the plants from frost, and during the day you can move them back into a warm spot.

The yardsticks used to measure vegetable climates differ from those used to measure the climates for vines, shrubs, and trees. With broadleafed evergreens, winter temperature is a most important factor in climate adaptation; but with vegetables, if the number of days between the last frost of spring and the first frost of fall totals enough for the vegetables you wish to grow, you can forget subzero winter temperatures.

We hope that the information on these pages and the following maps will help you understand the vegetable climate of your garden. The maps show you what zone you are in; the planting charts with the individual vegetables show you when to plant in that zone.

Because a climate will vary from one garden site to another within the same zone, precise directions are impossible to give. However, if you understand the zone's general climate characteristics, you will have the reference points you need to chart the special climate of your garden.

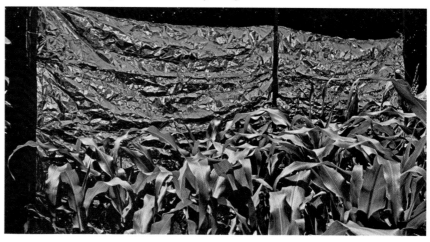

Gardeners with limited space and limited sunlight have found ingenious solutions to the problem. In this case aluminum foil was stapled to plastic and hung on both the east and west sides of the planted area. The results? The corn crop was perfect.

The Vegetable-Growing Climates of the South/Central States

The climate descriptions below correspond to the colored zones in the map on pages 24-25.

Zone 1

In the southern portion of Florida, the normal planting seasons of the northern states are reversed, starting with early spring for the cool-season vegetables. "Early spring" is September for broccoli, cabbage, lettuce, English peas, and potatoes. October is "spring planting time" for beets, carrots, radishes, spinach, and turnips. Tomatoes are a winter and summer crop, with a planting season from August to March. January is the starting date for the warm-weather vegetables such as pole beans, sweet corn, peppers, cucumbers, and the squash summer varieties.

Zone 2

The same preference for late-summer and fall plantings is found in the warmest portions of this zone. September is the best date for escarole, endive, lettuce, radishes, broccoli, and other cool-season crops.

There is winter frost in Zone 2, so don't plant snap beans, muskmelons, sweet corn, or peppers until the soil warms up in mid-February. Plant onions in September. Pick varieties to bulb in the short days of late winter and spring.

Zone 3

A long growing season of 260 days or more under the influence of the South Atlantic and Gulf Coasts gives the garden a definite spring and fall planting for the majority of crops. Plant broccoli, Brussels sprouts, Chinese cabbage, and kale in late summer—August and September. Plant warm-season crops early to avoid the hottest days and nights of summer.

Zone 4

There is considerable variation in climate from the southern to the northern portion of this zone. Plant cool-weather crops in mid-February. Delay plantings of muskmelons and squash until mid-March. A succession of plantings is possible for bush, snap, and lima beans—both in spring from mid-March through May, and again from July through mid-August.

Zone 5

The 200-day growing season here is long enough to allow summer plantings of snap beans, carrots, sweet corn, and tomatoes, as well as fall plantings of the cool-season crops.

Planting dates are a month later than in Zone 4. Get plantings for fall and winter harvest in by early August.

Zone 6

April 20 usually signals the last frost of spring, here. Inland areas have a fairly large number of clear days, while the coastal portions see less of the sun. The amount of rainfall varies greatly throughout the zone; the western area receives 20 inches or less of rain annually, while the eastern area along the coast gets twice that amount. As in Zone 5, the climate is versatile enough to allow spring and summer plantings of cool-season crops.

Zone 7

Here is the highest elevation in the South. It is also the shortest growing season—but there are about 160 growing days, more than enough to grow corn and tomatoes as well as a wide variety of both early spring and fall vegetables. You can plant lettuce, endive, turnips, Chinese cabbage, and kale in midsummer for fall and early winter harvest.

Zone 13

This zone covers the desert areas of Arizona, New Mexico and parts of Texas. As far as growing season and July temperatures can define a climate, the climates of zones 6 and 13 have much in common.

One of the specialities of the Southern growing region: sweet potatoes.

Vegetable-Growing Climates of the South/Central States (see page 23)

Zone 1
Southern Florida. Only intermittent freezes Dec. 15 through Feb. 1.

Zone 2
Growing season over 280 days. Last frost about Feb. 1.

Zone 3
Growing season around 260 days. Last frost about Feb. 20.

Zone 4
Growing season around 220 days. Last frost about Mar. 10.

Zone 5
Growing season around 200 days. Last frost about Mar. 25.

Zone 6
Growing season around 180 days. Last frost about Apr. 10.

Zone 7
Growing season around 160 days. Last frost about Apr. 30.

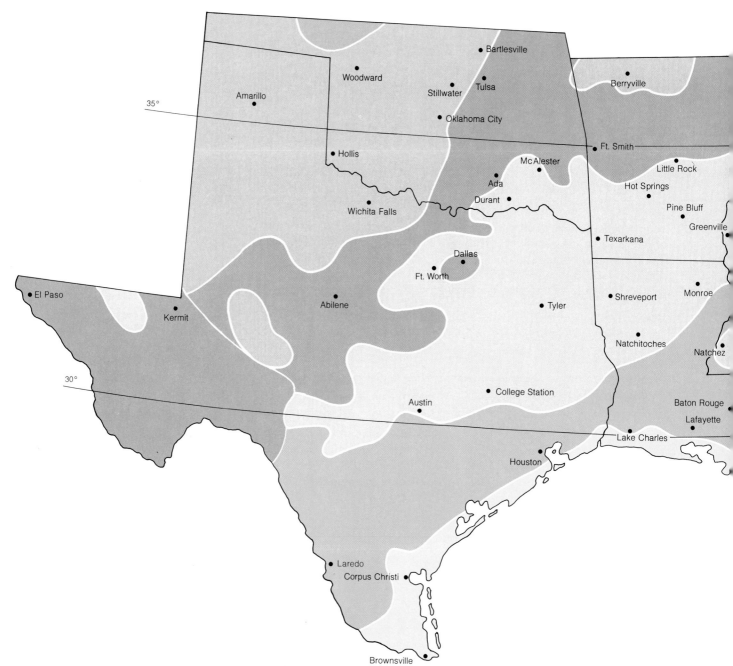

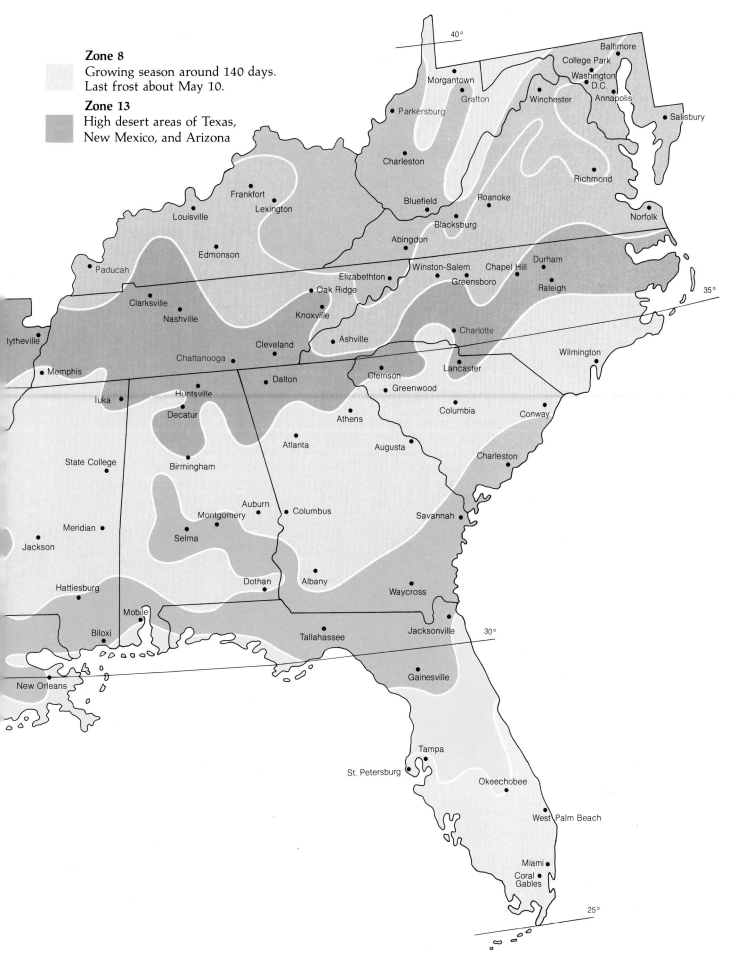

Zone 8
Growing season around 140 days.
Last frost about May 10.

Zone 13
High desert areas of Texas,
New Mexico, and Arizona

40°

35°

30°

25°

Baltimore
College Park
Washington
D.C.
Annapolis
Salisbury
Morgantown
Grafton
Winchester
Parkersburg
Richmond
Charleston
Frankfort
Bluefield
Roanoke
Lexington
Blacksburg
Louisville
Abingdon
Norfolk
Edmonson
Winston-Salem
Durham
Paducah
Elizabethton
Chapel Hill
Greensboro
Raleigh
Oak Ridge
Clarksville
Knoxville
Nashville
Charlotte
Cleveland
Ashville
Wilmington
lytheville
Chattanooga
Lancaster
Memphis
Dalton
Clemson
Greenwood
Iuka
Huntsville
Decatur
Athens
Columbia
Conway
Atlanta
State College
Augusta
Birmingham
Charleston
Auburn
Meridian
Montgomery
Columbus
Savannah
Jackson
Selma
Hattiesburg
Dothan
Albany
Waycross
Mobile
Biloxi
Tallahassee
Jacksonville
New Orleans
Gainesville
Tampa
St. Petersburg
Okeechobee
West Palm Beach
Miami
Coral
Gables

The Vegetable-Growing Climates in the Northern States

The climate descriptions below correspond to the colored zones in the map on pages 28-29.

Zone 5

These are the warmest areas along the southern borders of Missouri, Kentucky, and Virginia. The growing season, about 200 days, is long enough to allow summer plantings of snap beans, carrots, sweet corn, and tomatoes, as well as fall plantings of the cool-season crops.

Zone 6

April 20 usually signals the last frost of spring, here. Inland areas have a fairly high amount of clear days, while coastal portions see less sun. The amount of rainfall varies greatly throughout the zone. Parts of the western area receive only 20 inches of rain annually, while areas along the East Coast receive twice that amount. As in Zone 5, the climate is versatile enough to allow spring and summer plantings of cool-season crops. The summer season is long enough and temperatures are high enough to allow sweet potatoes to be grown commercially.

Zone 7

Stretching through the midsection of the northern region, this zone is great corn and tomato country and offers a wide choice of vegetables for both early spring and fall gardens. Take full advantage of the 160-day growing season by planting lettuce, endive, turnips, broccoli, Chinese cabbage, and kale in midsummer for fall and early winter harvest.

Zone 8

To make the most of this short but fast growing season of about 140 days, give the warm-season crops a head start by growing them from seed indoors, or by buying transplants to set out as soon as the warm weather arrives. Favor the early varieties of all long-season crops. The nights are cool enough to permit full-season crops.

A collection of winter squash in the cellar is an attractive and delicious reminder of a successful summer garden.

Zone 9

Gardeners in this zone find themselves pressed in a fairly short time period between spring and fall frost—about 120 days. Cool-season crops grow well here during the summer. Potatoes and rutabagas are among the vegetables that like it cool and thrive in this climate. Check the seed racks and catalogs for early, short-season varieties of the long-season crops, such as the midget muskmelons that ripen in 60 days, and early 'Sunglow' corn, which matures in 62 days.

Zone 10

Many vegetables fit this climate, although on the average there are only about 100 frost-free days. As in Zone 9, look for short-season varieties of long-season crops such as sweet corn, tomatoes, and melons. Use hot caps, clear plastic row covers, and black plastic mulch to extend the growing season (see page 50). Lettuce, cabbage, and other cool-season crops do well through the summer here.

Zone 11

Although the growing season is short—75 days or less—it is a merry one, with long warm days and cool nights. Canadian Experiment Stations have bred many vegetable varieties especially for this climate.

The Vegetable-Growing Climates of the West

The climate descriptions below correspond to the colored zones in the maps on pages 32 and 33.

Zone 6

Here are some of the best vegetable climates in the West. As in the Columbia River basin and the Lewiston and Boise valley areas in eastern Washington and Idaho, the growing season in this zone is longer and summer temperatures are higher than in Zone 8. Having a few degrees' higher temperatures, high light intensities, and low humidities, the areas build up enough total heat to grow melons successfully, even to grow okra and peanuts.

In Utah, the St. George area enjoys a 200-day growing season, with July temperatures averaging 78°. Salt Lake City has a growing season of 192 days, with July temperatures averaging 77°.

In Colorado, the growing season at Grand Junction is 191 days, with July temperatures averaging 78°. Pueblo gets 174 days, with the July average at 75°.

Zone 8

East of the Cascades and at lower elevations in the Rocky Mountain area, the growing season varies from 120 to 160 days. July temperatures of 66° to 72° are just right for the maximum growing of a wide variety of vegetables. Clear days, low humidities, and high light intensities favor rapid plant growth. From June through August, the area receives more than 80 percent of possible sunshine. In the shortest growing season, favor the early maturing varieties of the warm-season crops.

Zone 9

Gardeners in this zone find themselves pressed in a fairly short time period between spring and fall frost—about 120 days. Cool-season crops grow well here during the summer. Potatoes and rutabagas are among the vegetables that like it cool and thrive in this climate. Check the seed racks and catalogs for early, short-season varieties of the long-season crops, such as the midget muskmelons that ripen in 60 days, and early 'Sunglow' corn, which matures in 62 days.

Zone 10

Many vegetables fit this climate, although on the average there are only about 100 frost-free days. As in Zone 9, look for short-season varieties of long-season crops such as sweet corn, tomatoes, and melons. Use hot caps, clear plastic

In areas where the weather is sufficiently cold, many root crops can be stored in the ground for winter use. A thick (12 to 18 inch) layer of straw mulch over the ground before the first snow will keep the ground from freezing, and ensures easy digging

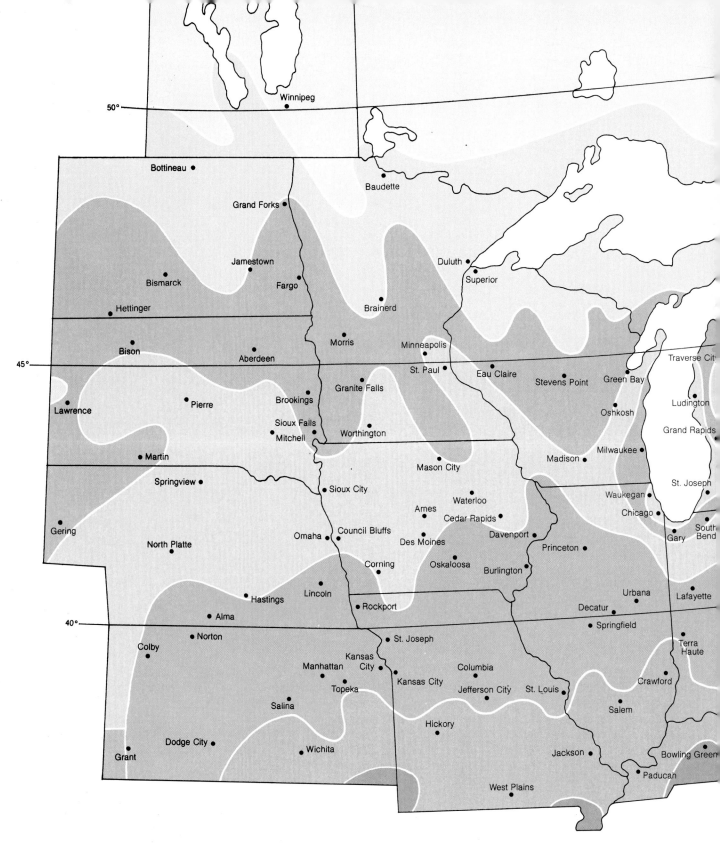

Vegetable-Growing Climates of the Northern States (see pages 26-27)

Zone 5
Growing season around 200 days.
Last frost about Mar. 25.

Zone 6
Growing season around 180 days.
Last frost about Apr. 10.

Zone 7
Growing season around 160 days.
Last frost about Apr. 30.

Zone 8
Growing season around 140 days.
Last frost about May 10.

Zone 9

Growing season around 120 days.
Last frost about May 15.

Zone 10

Growing season around 100 days.
Last frost about May 20.

Zone 11

Growing season 75 days or less.
Last frost June 1 or later.

Zone 12

High elevations of western mountains.
Growing season 60 to 120 days.

The West is blessed with some of the best growing climates in the United States. Legendary tales of abundance are what brought many of the original settlers to the area.

row covers, and black plastic mulch to extend the growing season (see page 50). Lettuce, cabbage, and other cool-season crops do well through the summer here.

Zone 12

This zone has extreme variations in elevations and growing seasons. Spring weather may fluctuate from subfreezing at night to the upper 60s and 70s in midafternoon. Many areas have a 120-day growing season; others have less than 60 frost-free days; and some can expect frost every month of the year.

In the 100-day areas, the last frost date in spring occurs around May 30. July temperatures average 58° to 66°.

In these high-elevation areas, you can successfully grow sweet corn, winter squash, peppers, and other long-season leafy vegetables that can be harvested before they are mature. Most root crops—turnips, carrots, beets and potatoes —give good yields.

Zone 13

This zone covers the desert areas of Arizona and New Mexico. As far as growing season and July temperatures can define a climate, the climates of Zones 6 and 13 have much in common. Here's how they look statistically:

City	Growing Season	Av. July Temp.
Salt Lake City, Utah	192	77°
Grand Junction, Col.	191	78°
Albuquerque, N.M.	198	78°
Roswell, N.M.	207	78°
Douglas, Ariz.	212	80°
Kingman, Ariz.	212	82°

In all these areas, the last frost of spring is between April 8 and April 13.

However, in the high desert areas of New Mexico and Arizona, high summer temperatures in the more than 100° range occur much more often, and the desert winds must be considered as well. The end of the growing season is not abrupt, and the fall garden is a better bet.

Zone 14

The low and intermediate desert areas of Arizona are extensions of the low deserts of California. In growing vegetables, however, there is no sharp line between the low and intermediate deserts. In both the planting season begins in September. The hardy vegetables coast through the winter months; those that can't take frost are started early in the year so that they can mature before the high temperatures of July and August arrive.

Zone 15

The intermediate and high desert areas of California have a special blend of climates, from the low desert in the southern portion to the high elevations in the north. The climate varies so greatly that you'll probably need a year of experience to know how to make the most of your growing season. If your garden is in the Lancaster, Mojave, or China Lake areas, you can consider April to November as your growing season, although a freak April frost is a possibility. The wind storms of spring and early summer are a hazard. Temperatures of 106° to 108° in July and August stop the blossom set on beans and tomatoes. However, the total summer heat is much less than that of the low desert. Hot days are followed by cool nights.

Zone 16

The cool summer climates of western Washington and Oregon make up this zone. The climate of Seattle and Tacoma is typical: the growing season is 250 to 255 days, with the last frost of spring March 13 or 14 and the first frost of fall as late as November 18 to 24. But summer temperatures are low, with a July average of only 63°. From June through August, this area receives less than 60 percent of possible sunshine. It's a great climate for the cool-season vegetables, but only the early varieties of corn and tomatoes are sure to ripen. The length of the growing season partially offsets its coolness. Low temperatures and rain in October put an end to the tomato season before the first frosts of fall.

Zone 17

Here is a slightly warmer version of Zone 16. The Portland and Willamette Valley areas have higher summer temperatures, more days of sunshine, and distance from the ocean, so they allow a wider choice of warm-weather crops.

The Portland area has a growing season of 260 days, with the last frosts of spring in early April and the first frosts of fall in late November. July temperatures average 67°. Albany, Corvallis, and Eugene have a shorter growing season—from 200 to 212 days—with the last frost date from April 4 to 15. However, July temperatures average 66° to 67°.

Zone 18

The coastal areas of Northern California to San Luis Obispo are more or less directly influenced by the ocean fogs. South of San Francisco is lettuce and artichoke country, plus all of the cool-weather crops thrown in for good measure. The possibility of sunshine for the summer in San Francisco is 69 percent.

The flow of marine air is not uniform. Where the fog cover is broken by land forms, there are several consistently open areas where summer temperatures increase and warm-weather vegetables are grown.

Zone 19

This zone covers the Southern California coastal region, from Santa Barbara to San Diego. The lima bean was once typical of this climate, being a vegetable that requires a season of modest warmth and no hot dry winds. The pattern of marine air flow is not uniform. Summer warmth varies greatly because of local fog patterns.

Zone 20

This zone includes the valleys north and south of San Francisco, which are partially influenced by the ocean. Summer temperatures are consistently higher than in Zone 18, and the warm-weather crops—corn, tomatoes, and peppers—thrive here. The daytime midsummer temperatures in the Santa Rosa and St. Helena areas range from 80° to 90°, as compared to 77° to 83° in the Santa Clara Valley. Normal winters are mild enough for a fall and winter garden of hardy crops.

Zone 21

From the viewpoint of a subtropical plant, this climate should be divided into 50 climate zones, varying from one with marine influence to one with a near-desert climate. But from the vegetable gardener's viewpoint, it's ideal vegetable country. Most of the area enjoys more than 300 frost-free days.

Zone 22

A long growing season of about 270 days, with high summer temperatures and 95 percent possible sunshine in summer, creates the ideal growing season in this zone for the high-sugar crenshaw, honeydew, casaba, and Persian melons. The spring gardening season from February to June is the time for cool-weather crops. Low temperatures and ground fog discourage winter gardening.

Long hot growing seasons produce crops with the taste of summer sunshine. Peppers can be used for decorative purposes as well as for seasoning.

Vegetable-Growing Climates of California and the Western States

(see pages 27, 30, 31)

Zone 6
Growing season around 180 days.
Last frost about Apr. 10.

Zone 8
Growing season around 140 days.
Last frost about May 10.

Zone 9
Growing season around 120 days.
Last frost about May 15.

Zone 10
Growing season around 100 days.
Last frost about May 20.

Zone 12
High elevations of western mountains.
Growing season 60 to 120 days.

Zone 13
High desert areas of Texas,
New Mexico, and Arizona.

Zone 14
Low to intermediate deserts of
Arizona and low deserts of California.

Zone 15
High and intermediate deserts
of California.

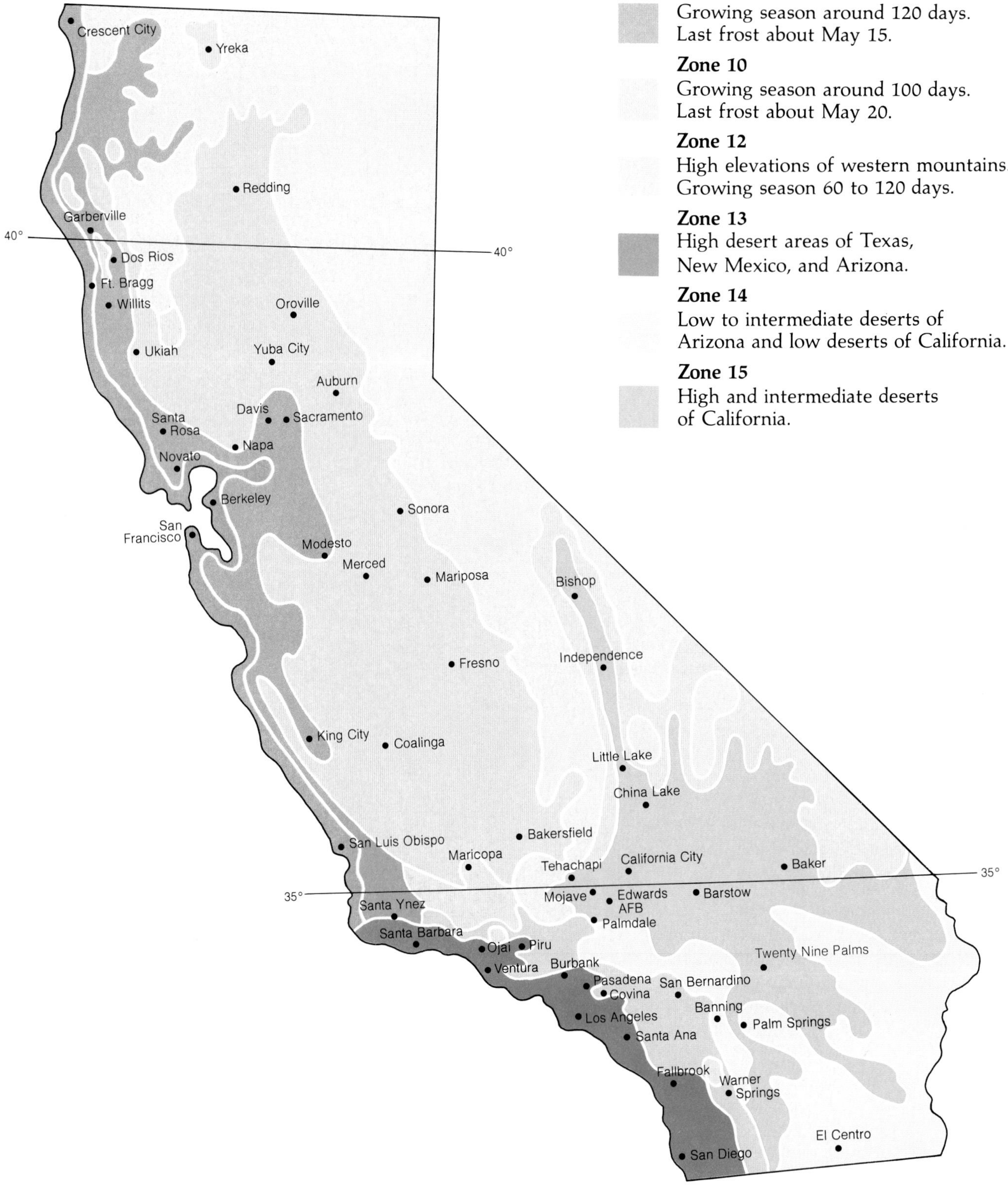

Crescent City
Yreka
Redding
Garberville
40°   40°
Dos Rios
Ft. Bragg
Willits
Oroville
Ukiah
Yuba City
Auburn
Davis
Santa Rosa   Sacramento
Novato   Napa
Berkeley
San Francisco   Sonora
Modesto
Merced   Mariposa
Bishop
Fresno   Independence
King City   Coalinga
Little Lake
China Lake
San Luis Obispo   Bakersfield
Maricopa
Tehachapi   California City   Baker
35°   35°
Santa Ynez   Mojave   Edwards AFB   Barstow
Santa Barbara   Palmdale
Ojai   Piru
Ventura   Burbank   Twenty Nine Palms
Pasadena   San Bernardino
Covina
Los Angeles   Banning
Santa Ana   Palm Springs
Fallbrook   Warner Springs
El Centro
San Diego

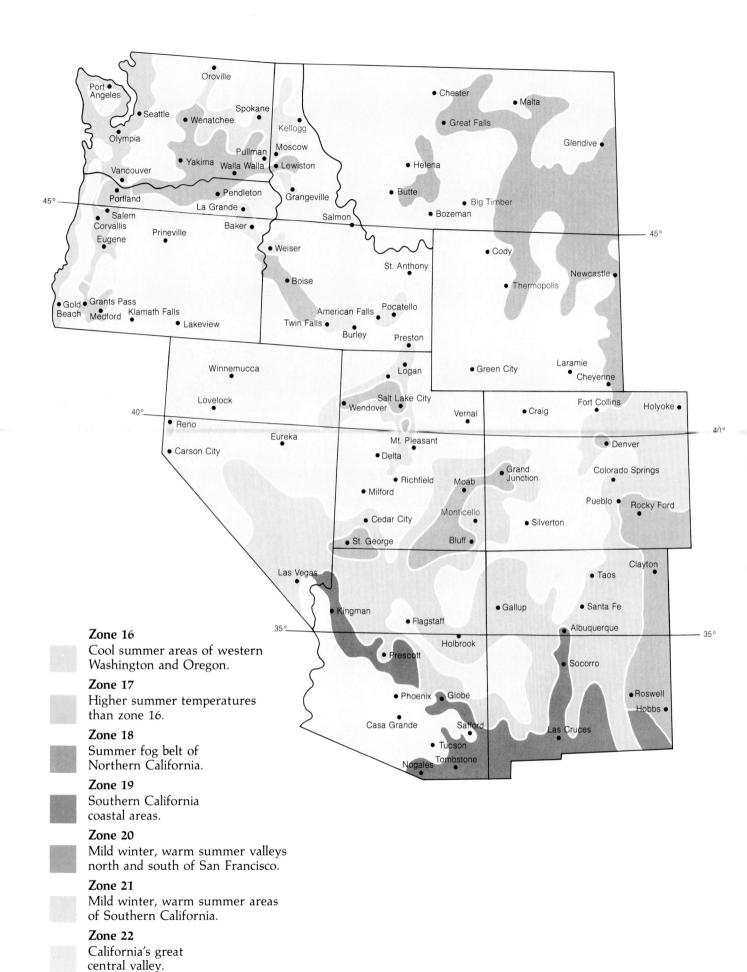

Port
Angeles •

• Oroville

• Chester

• Malta

• Seattle   • Wenatchee   Spokane
                              •

Olympia •

Kellogg

• Great Falls

Glendive •

Vancouver •

Moscow
•

Yakima   Pullman
  •   •   • Lewiston
     Walla Walla

Helena
•

45° ——   • Portland   • Pendleton

  • Salem
Corvallis •   La Grande •

• Grangeville

Butte
•

Big Timber
•

—— 45°

Eugene •   Prineville
  •   •

Baker •

Salmon

Bozeman
•

• Weiser

St. Anthony
•

Cody
•

Newcastle
•

Gold • Grants Pass
Beach • Medford Klamath Falls
                    •   • Lakeview

• Boise

American Falls   Pocatello
   •   •
Twin Falls •
        Burley •
             Preston •

Thermopolis
•

Logan
•

Green City
•

Laramie
•
    Cheyenne •

Winnemucca
•

Lovelock
•

Salt Lake City
•
Wendover •

Vernal
•

• Craig

Fort Collins
•

Holyoke
•

40° —— • Reno

Eureka
•

Mt. Pleasant
•
 • Delta

—— 40°

• Carson City

• Denver

Richfield
•   Moab
Milford •   •

Grand
Junction •

Colorado Springs
•

Cedar City
•
    St. George •

Monticello
•

Bluff
•

Pueblo
• Rocky Ford
•

• Silverton

Clayton
•

Las Vegas
•

Taos
•

Kingman
•
     Flagstaff
      •

Gallup
•

Santa Fe
•

35° ——   Holbrook
                  •

Albuquerque
•

—— 35°

Prescott
•

Socorro
•

Phoenix Globe
 •   •

Roswell
•
   Hobbs
   •

Casa Grande
•

Safford
•

Las Cruces
•

Tucson
•
Nogales Tombstone
  •   •

Zone 16
Cool summer areas of western
Washington and Oregon.

Zone 17
Higher summer temperatures
than zone 16.

Zone 18
Summer fog belt of
Northern California.

Zone 19
Southern California
coastal areas.

Zone 20
Mild winter, warm summer valleys
north and south of San Francisco.

Zone 21
Mild winter, warm summer areas
of Southern California.

Zone 22
California's great
central valley.

CLIMATE AND GARDENING / 33

THE BASICS OF VEGETABLE GARDENING

The basic information anyone needs to know to grow good vegetables can be found in this chapter. Take time to read it and future rewards from the garden will be practically guaranteed.

As much as some people would have you believe otherwise, gardening is not an exact science that takes considerable time to understand. In most cases, there is considerable latitude in the care and treatment any plant is willing to receive and still grow satisfactorily. What is very important, though, is an understanding of the basics: soil, water, fertilizers, and the fundamentals of plant growth. If you read and digest the information in the following chapter you'll be well on your way to becoming a good gardener.

Soil

Soils can be looked at from two viewpoints: that of the container gardener, who's planning to grow vegetables in some kind of container, and that of the dirt gardener, who wants to prepare a plot of ground for vegetables.

The Dirt Gardener

If you have ever read the planting directions on a seed packet or a catalog, you are familiar with such instructions as "Sow seed in early spring as soon as the soil can be worked," and "Plant in a well-drained sandy loam." But how *early* is "as soon as the ground can be worked" in your garden? If your rain-soaked, heavy clay soil isn't ready for spading or tilling until summer, you won't be able to take advantage of spring—the best growing season for such crops as peas and lettuce.

Why do you need "good drainage"? When water replaces air in the soil, roots suffocate; they will not develop unless oxygen is supplied constantly and carbon dioxide is removed constantly. What is a well-drained soil? One in which the water moves through quickly, without ever completely shutting off the movement of air through the soil.

A sandy soil is well drained, but it dries out quickly. Watering a sandy soil frequently washes nutrients right through the soil.

The best advice we can give is: "Don't try to live with an unfavorable soil." Nothing can dampen a beginner's enthusiasm more quickly than a hard-to-manage soil. And the only quick way to change either a heavy clay soil or a light sandy soil into a rich-loam soil is by adding organic matter—not just a little, but lots of it.

The addition of organic matter—compost, peat moss, manure, sawdust, or ground bark—makes clay soils more mellow and easy to work. Organic matter opens up tight clay soils, improves drainage, and allows air to move more readily through the soil, which warms it up earlier in spring. In light sandy soils, organic matter holds moisture and nutrients in the root zone.

However, adding huge doses of organic matter to the soil is not the same as a long-term improvement program. It is the latter that causes the breakdown of organic matter into true humus—that final, black, sticky material that holds soil particles together in crumbs.

You must add enough organic matter to change the physical structure of the

The camera catches the critical moment in the birth of a bean (top) as it pulls the swollen seed, now heavy with water, through the soil. Then the seedling breaks through and spreads its pair of primary leaves.

soil. "Enough" means that at least 1/3 of the final mix should be organic matter.

To add this amount, spread a layer of organic matter over the soil at least 2 inches thick and work it in to a depth of 4 inches.

Add the organic matter when you're preparing the soil for planting. Spread the normal amount of fertilizer over the organic material (4 to 5 pounds of 5-10-10 per 100 square feet) and till it into the soil very thoroughly (see page 40). If you use peat moss, add ground limestone at the rate of 5 pounds per 100 square feet.

If you add raw sawdust that has not been composted or fortified with nitrogen, you will have to increase the amount of fertilizer to protect against the bacteria that attack the sawdust. If you don't add nitrogen to the sawdust, the bacteria will rob the soil of nitrogen while breaking down the sawdust.

So for every 10 cubic feet of sawdust, add ½ pound of actual nitrogen. That means 10 pounds of 5-10-10, or 4 pounds of blood meal. And that means 18 pounds of 5-10-10 per 100 square feet of sawdust 2 inches thick.

Preparing the soil in individual planting holes is a good way to add organic matter. When setting out a few plants of tomatoes, eggplants, peppers, melons, cucumbers, or zucchini, dig a hole for each plant. Just for good measure, put a shovelful of manure at the bottom of the hole. Make a 50-50 mix of the top soil and peat moss, and backfill the mix.

If your soil is heavy clay and water doesn't drain through it, the planting hole may become a bathtub in which the plant will drown. In problem soils like this, plant above ground in raised beds.

The No-Soil Gardener

If you are a mini-gardener, a roof-top gardener, or a pot/box/tub gardener, you can buy soil substitutes or synthetic soils in garden stores. These substitutes have many advantages over real soil. They are clean; they are free of weed seeds and plant-disease organisms; and they are very lightweight—containers filled with these synthetic soils are easy to move.

As a growing medium for vegetables, the mixes are almost foolproof. They can scarcely be waterlogged—excess water drains through rapidly. Plant roots spread throughout the well-aerated soil, rather than developing at the edge of the containers.

Cornell and the University of California pioneered in formulating standard "soil" mixes for commercial plant growers. Mixes that follow these formulas are available under several labels. Some of the nationally distributed brands are "Jiffy Mix," "Redi Earth," and "Pro-Mix." In the West, several companies package the U.C.-type mix under such brands as "First Step" and "Super Soil."

The basic difference between the original U.C. mix and the Cornell version is that the Cornell mix uses vermiculite and the U.C. mix uses fine sand.

In small containers, you can use the mixes straight; in large containers and raised beds, you can extend them with garden soil.

You can make your own "soil" mix. If you plan to fill a few planter boxes, a half-dozen large pots, or a raised bed, mix the largest amount that you can handle easily in one mixing operation—about a cubic yard, or 27 cubic feet. Make the mix of equal amounts of peat moss and vermiculite. Peat moss comes in 6-cubic-foot bales; vermiculite comes in 4-cubic-foot bags. So buy 2 bales of peat moss and 3 bags of vermiculite and call it a yard. The peat moss will expand to more than make up the difference between 24 and 27 cubic feet.

Dampen the peat moss and mix it roughly with the vermiculite. Over the pile, spread: 6 pounds of 5-10-10 commercial fertilizer (see the section on fertilizers, page 40); 2 pounds of superphosphate; and 5 pounds of agricultural lime. Then mix, mix, and mix again.

The best way to mix is first to shovel the rough mix into a cone-shaped pile, allowing each shovelful to run down the cone as it builds up. (See illustration.)

If you need less mix than the above recipe offers, cut down on all elements in proportion.

Composting

Why compost? To convert waste material into a sort of synthetic manure—dark brown crumbly stuff with that good-earth fragrance.

How to compost? Take leaves, grass clippings, small prunings, straw, spoiled hay, sawdust, green weeds, dry weeds, vegetable harvest refuse, vegetable matter from the kitchen, coffee grounds, eggshells, shredded paper, and/or wood ashes, and pile them up. Soil bacteria will thrive, multiply, and break down these waste materials into a form you can use.

In order to convert the raw material, bacteria need a suitable environment to work in—moisture, air, and food.

Grass clippings, green weeds, lettuce leaves, pea vines, and other succulent materials contain sugar and proteins, which are excellent nutrients for the bacteria. They decompose rapidly—sometimes too rapidly. However, dry leaves, small twigs, sawdust, and similar woody, dry materials decompose very slowly, unless the bacteria are supplied with extra nitrogen.

The particle size of the woody material affects the rate of decomposition. If large and small leaves are put into the pile intact as they are raked up, decomposition will be much slower than if the leaves are shredded by a rotary mower.

Prunings, clippings, and wood chips will take months to break down, even with extra nitrogen. However, if you put them through a shredder and mix them with green material, they will decompose rapidly.

If you have a lot of grass clippings, mix them thoroughly into the composting material to avoid odor and fly problems. A good load of fine grass clippings will not decay normally but will make a soggy mass, putrify, and become an unexpected incubator for fly eggs. After you've mixed the clippings into the compost, spread a layer of soil or old compost over the top.

Adding Organic Material

The following table shows how much sawdust or other organic material you would need to cover 100 square feet at various depths.

Depth	To cover 100 Sq. Ft.
6"	2 cu. yds.
4	35 cu. ft.
3	1 cu. yd.
2	18 cu. ft.
1	9 cu. ft.
1/4	2 cu. ft.
1/8	1 cu. ft.
1 cubic yard = 27 cubic feet	

Store bought soil mixes contain these ingredients . . .

Making Your Own Soil Mix

You can make your own soil mix by using one of the formulas in the text and mixing it very thoroughly. By "very thoroughly" we mean that it must be mixed so each portion, even a 2" potful, has the proper portions of each ingredient. To mix it well follow these steps:

1. Pour the dampened peat moss and perlite or vermiculite in a rough pile. Sprinkle the fertilizer and lime on top.
2. Shoveling from the first pile, make a cone-shaped pile by pouring each shovelful directly on top so ingredients dribble down the sides.
3. Shovel from the second pile and repeat the cone-shaped pile building and dribbling.
4. Do it again. Make a third cone-shaped pile. It's then ready to use.

Compost Bins

Here are several easy ways to construct a serviceable compost pile.

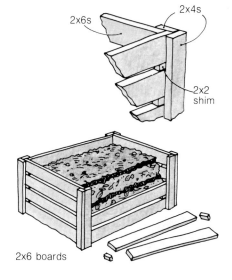

2x6s
2x4s
2x2 shim

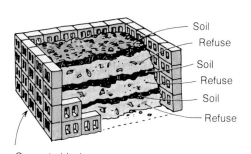

2x6 boards

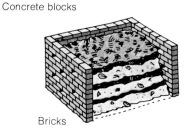

Soil
Refuse
Soil
Refuse
Soil
Refuse

Concrete blocks

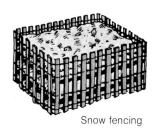

Bricks

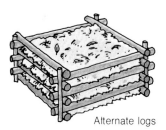

Snow fencing

Alternate logs

The Classic Layer Cake

Experienced gardeners know that the best way to build a compost pile is to stack up layers of waste material, putting fertilizers, manures, and garden soil between the layers.

Although the size of the pile will depend on the size of your garden, it is easier to manage two 4-by-6 piles than one 4-by-12 pile.

Start the pile by spreading a 6- to 8-inch-thick layer of refuse over the 4- by 6-foot area. Over this layer, spread a mixture of manure, garden soil, and commercial fertilizers. This is the filling on the layer cake; and the composition of this filling can cause some debate among composters.

You do need to use both manure and a commercial fertilizer to give the bacteria the food they need. If the waste material is dry rather than green, you'll need to use more fertilizer. The more you use, the richer your compost will be. A good average amount is 2 cupfuls of ammonium sulfate or blood meal for each layer.

Wet down the fertilizer layer just enough for the water to carry the chemicals through the layer — not so heavily that you wash them out altogether.

If your soil is on the acid side, add a cupful of ground limestone, crushed oyster shell, or dolomite lime to each layer to make the soil less acid and improve decomposition as well.

Now add another layer of vegetable matter, spread the soil-manure-chemical layer over it, and wet it down. Repeat the layering process until you either run out of material or have a 4- to 5-foot-high pile.

Form a basin at the top for watering and catching rain.

Keep the pile as wet as a squeezed-out sponge. If your climate is dry, in warm weather you may need to water as often as every 4 to 5 days. **Under normal conditions**, you should turn the pile in 2 or 3 weeks, and again in 5 weeks. It should be ready to use in 3 months.

However, you can shorten that time to a few weeks if you put the material through a shredder before you build the pile. Since more surface is exposed to decay bacteria, the smaller pieces decompose faster. Shredding also makes a fluffier mixture, which allows more efficient air and water penetration.

If you build the pile when the weather is warm, in 24 to 30 hours you'll see heat waves rising above the pile. Turn the pile to mix the material, and water thoroughly. It will heat up again, and in a few days it will be hot enough to require turning once more. Each time you turn it, move the outer materials toward the center, where heat and moisture encourage decomposition.

One advantage to the fast, high-heat method of composting is that it destroys most of the weed seeds.

To get the most benefit out of composting, it pays to have 3 piles going: one in which the compost is ready to use as a synthetic manure; another that furnishes partially decomposed material for mulching; and a third that's working in the first stages of the recycling process.

Water

Watering—this subject is the most difficult to understand, the most frustrating, and the most confusing.

Ask why the tomato blossoms drooped and you are told that you applied either too much or too little water. Ask why the carrots are stumpy and you are warned against overwatering. Ask why the lettuce is bitter and you are cautioned against giving an uneven supply of water.

But what's "too much"? What's "too little"? "Too much water" can mean (1) too much water for the roots to grow in, or (2) an oversupply of water (moisture), giving the plant maximum *leaf* growth, instead of *fruit* growth.

Water has been called the "hazardous necessity," meaning that you can kill a plant with water. Plant roots require moisture and air for growth; they require a growing medium that air can move through to bring oxygen and remove carbon dioxide.

If you fill all the air spaces in the soil with water, you stop the supply of air —and root growth stops. The longer that air is cut off, the greater the damage to the roots. And since damaged roots have little defense against the entrance of rot-causing soil organisms, the plant dies of root rot.

The planting directions for the various vegetables proclaim more warnings: "Plant in a well-drained, rich loamy soil," or "Does best in a light, well-drained soil."

Such warnings mean that too much water will damage the plant.

As you develop good watering habits, you will learn to apply water according to the nature of your own soil. There is no way to half-wet the soil—you have to go all the way. But you can prevent overwatering by fitting the intervals between watering to the water-holding capacity of your soil.

Clay soils have a high water-holding capacity; the air spaces are minute, and water moves through them slowly.

Such soils need watering only infrequently. If you have clay soil, you'll learn to use "the spade test"—to look at and feel the soil beneath the surface inches.

The very best way to solve the problem of water management is to prepare a garden soil that can't be overwatered. See "Soil," page 34.

Irrigation specialists have coined a useful term: they say that a plant that is not getting its full quota of water is under *water stress*. As the moisture supply in the soil decreases, the plant must work harder. Stress is progressive, slight to severe.

Water stress will produce a quick flowering of annual flowers in a dry spell. When growing herbs for a seed crop, it is normal to put the plant under water stress to produce seeds more quickly.

In the vegetable garden, however, water stress is something you *don't* want

Individual compost piles will produce widely different results, depending on what originally went into the pile. Although compost rarely is considered a complete fertilizer, it frequently contains the essential nutrients for plant growth. Of course, it's also an excellent soil amendment.

Critical Watering Periods

It's difficult to say when watering is most critical in the life of any vegetable. A report from Rutgers says that watering is most necessary for successful harvesting of the crop during the following periods:

Vegetable	Critical Period
Asparagus	Brush—Fern
Broccoli	Head development
Cabbage	Head development
Carrot	Root enlargement
Cauliflower	Head development
Corn	Silking and tasseling, ear development
Cucumber	Flowering and fruit development
Eggplant	Flowering and fruit development
Lettuce	Head development
Lima bean	Pollination and pod development
Melon	Flowering and fruit development
Onion, dry	Bulb enlargement

Right: Water is concentrated in the root zone of this bush-type zucchini using a bottomless coffee can sunk in the ground.

Far right: Notice the deep furrow on the right of the melon plants. This type of irrigation allows the soil to be thoroughly watered without wetting the surrounding soil. Vines are trained away from the furrow so that melons are on dry ground.

Percentage of Nitrogen Affects Application Rates

Formula	Pounds per 100 sq. ft.
5-10-10	3.5
6-20-10	2.8
8-24-8	2.0
10-10-8	1.7
16-16-15	1.0

—except on rare occasions, such as if your tomato plant is only producing vines.

Water stress affects various vegetables in special ways. When cucumber is under stress, it just stops growing; but when it receives water, it resumes growth.

When tomatoes are put under stress, they will ripen all their fruits as they near harvesting size.

Lettuce needs a steady supply of moisture; and since it has a shallow root system, you'll have to water frequently.

If muskmelons experience water stress during their ripening period, they lose their sweetness.

Unlike flowers, vegetables never fully recover from a severe check in growth due to lack of water.

Wind protection in the vegetable garden pays off in several ways. Wind breaks keep water loss down; avert physical damage to plants; and remove one negative factor from the destructive combination of high temperatures, high light intensity, low humidities, and strong winds.

Remember too, that vegetable seedlings compete with weeds for the existing water supply—and come off poorly in the contest.

It's important to use a summer mulch of organic matter in maintaining a steady supply of moisture. See pages 16-19 about mulches.

Fertilizers

The gardeners we worked with through the year handled their fertilizing program in many—and sometimes strange—ways. They used every type of product, from fish, blood meal, and manure to commercial liquid and dry fertilizers. They talked about overfertilizing tomatoes and peppers and underfeeding cabbage. In three different locations where manure was free and easily available, they had a problem with salt buildup in the soil.

In using fertilizer, the first step is to understand the label on bags and packages.

All commercial fertilizers are labeled according to the percentages of nitrogen, phosphorus, and potassium (N, P, K) they contain. There are many formulas—4-12-4, 5-10-10, 6-20-10, 10-10-10 and so on—but the listings are always in the same order, with nitrogen first. The numbers refer to the number of pounds of each element in 100 pounds of the fertilizer. The amount of nitrogen in the formula dictates the amount of fertilizer to apply; the phosphorus and potassium just tag along. If your fertilizer has a higher percentage of nitrogen, use less of it. If you don't read the directions on the package, you may apply 2 or 3 times more nitrogen than you should.

The chart at left shows how the amount to be applied decreases as the percentage of nitrogen increases. (Assume that fertilizer recommendations call for 3 to 4 pounds per 100 square feet.)

If you use liquid measurements when applying fertilizer, you can easily figure out the amount to apply per square foot or length of row. A pint is a pound, 1 cup is ½ pound, and so on.

Ways To Apply Dry Fertilizers

(1) Mix dry fertilizer with the soil before planting. Spread the fertilizer evenly over the soil at the rate called for on the fertilizer bag or box, and work it into the soil with a spade or power tiller.

(2) Apply dry fertilizer in narrow bands of furrows that are 2 to 3 inches from the seed and 1 to 2 inches deeper than you intend to place the seeds or plants.

If you carelessly place the band too close to the seeds, the roots of the seedlings will get burned. The best way is to stretch a string where you intend to plant the seed row. Then, with a corner of a hoe, dig a furrow 3 inches deep, and 3 inches to one side of and parallel to the string. Spread the fertilizer in the furrow and cover it with soil. Repeat the banding operation on the other side of the string. Then sow the seeds underneath the strings.

For widely spaced plants such as tomatoes, you can place fertilizers in bands 6 inches long for each plant, or in a circle around the plant. Make the bands 4 inches from the plant base.

(3) Apply dry fertilizer as a side-dressing, after the plants are up and growing. Scatter it on both sides of the row, 6 to 8 inches from the plants; rake it into the soil; and water thoroughly. Banding is one way to satisfy the need that many plants, especially tomatoes, have for a supply of phosphorus as the first roots develop. If you broadcast fertilizer and work it into the soil, the soil locks up much of the phosphorus, so the plant can't use it immediately. But if you concentrate the phosphorus in the band, the plant gets what it needs, even though much of the application is locked up.

Another way to satisfy the plant's need for phosphorus is to use a "starter solution" when you set out transplants of tomatoes, eggplant, peppers, or cabbage. You can use any liquid fertilizer that's high in phosphorus as a starter solution. Just follow the directions on the label.

You also can make your own starter solution with the fertilizer you are using, if it is high in phosphorus. When using 5-10-10, dissolve 1 pound in 5 gallons of water. It won't dissolve completely; you'll have to stir it while you use it. Place the transplant in the planting hole, fill the hole half full of soil, pour in a cupful of the solution, and fill the hole with soil up to the top.

Take it easy with all types of fertilizers. Too much manure can cause as much trouble as too much of any other kind of fertilizer. Cut down on the rate of fertilizers when you use manure.

With liquid fertilizers, follow the label directions.

Follow up dry fertilizer applications with a good watering to dissolve the fertilizer and carry it into the root zone.

When using large amounts of fertilizer for heavy feeders such as cabbage and onions, apply half the amount before planting and sidedress with the remainder once the growth is underway.

Check the timing for applying fertilizer for each vegetable. The first application, aimed to produce early vigorous leaf growth, is all-important with many crops. The yield of bush snap beans, for example, depends upon how big the plant is before flowering starts.

Plants grown in partial shade require less nitrogen than the recommended same kind of plants grown in full sun.

Increase the amount of fertilizer when crowding plants by narrowing the spacing between the rows, and when growing them in a solid block pattern rather than in rows.

Fertilizer banding when planting seeds.

1" 2" to 3"

Side dressing fertilizer on established plants.

When transplanting, firm the soil around the rootball, water to settle the soil . . .

Fill any settled area with more soil mix.

Vegetable growing offers a variety of
rewards: the practicality of raised beds, the
pleasant geometry of vegetables in rows,
and the added elegance of
turf-covered paths.

PLANNING THE GARDEN

"Make a good plan before you plant" is good advice, particularly to novice gardeners. Planning means knowing what you're going to plant, how much you're going to plant, and where you're going to plant it.

We asked our panel of first-year vegetable gardeners what mistakes they'd made in planning their gardens. With almost one voice, they responded, "We got too much of one thing at one time.... We grew more squash than we could give away."

It isn't easy to plan for a continuous supply of fresh vegetables—neither too much nor too little. And it's even more difficult for the limited-space gardener than for the farm-space gardener.

In the farm garden, after all, you can block out space for the spring garden and hold back space for the summer garden. By the time the spring garden is harvested, you can plant the fall garden. But if you garden on a city or suburban lot, you have no such space options. You have to plant everything in the space you've got. In the face of such limitations, you may get carried away by enthusiasm when the first spring planting comes. Having prepared your 20- by 30-foot piece of ground, you may buy a dozen packets of seeds, each one of which will give you 50 or 100 feet of row.

Before you actually plant, you easily could conclude that 20 or 30 heads of lettuce might not be enough to feed your family—after all, that 30-foot row can look pretty short. But when 30 heads come into the kitchen within 10 days, you begin to realize that a short row can produce a long supply of vegetables.

A dozen cabbage plants nestling in little trays at the nursery can look quite innocent—but when 36 to 40 pounds of cabbage come through your kitchen door, you'll need to learn how to make sauerkraut.

Fortunately, not all vegetables have short harvest periods. And regarding those that do, if you select two or three varieties of the short-harvest kinds, you can spread the harvest period out. (See text on cabbage and corn for examples, pages 81 and 89.)

Vegetables With A Long Harvest Period

Some vegetables provide a long harvest period by storing well in the soil. These include carrots, beets, parsnips, salsify, and Florence fennel. Carrots and beets yield a succession of harvests—from baby beets and carrots up to mature size —which then can be stored for weeks or months, depending upon the time of year and the storage conditions. Leaf lettuce and Swiss chard can be picked a leaf at a time.

Make a succession of plantings. One answer to the feast-and-famine problem is to make successive plantings of small quantities.

For example, if you make your first planting of lettuce in March, make another planting in April, and then another in May. If you plant snap beans in succession, 4 to 6 weeks apart, you will have fresh beans for 5 months or more.

To get a continuous harvest of a vegetable, you must put in the second planting before you harvest the first. But how is the small-space gardener to find room for the second or third planting?

Early Spring

Plant as soon as ground can be worked in spring: Broccoli plants, Cabbage plants, Endive, Kohlrabi, Lettuce, Onion sets, Parsley, Peas, Radishes, Spinach, Turnips.

Mid-Spring

Plant these at time of the average last killing frost: Carrots, Cauliflower plants, Beets, Onion seeds, Parsnips, Swiss Chard. Plant two weeks later: Beans, Corn, Potatoes, Early Tomato seeds.

Early Summer

Plant when soil and weather are warm: Lima Beans, Cantaloupe, Celery plants, Crenshaw melons, Cucumbers, Eggplant plants, Pumpkins, Pepper plants, Potatoes for winter, Squash, Tomato plants, Watermelons.

Mid-Summer-Fall

Plant in late June or early July: Beets, Broccoli, Cabbage, Cauliflower, Kohlrabi, Lettuce, Radishes, Spinach, Turnips.

When garden planning is concentrated on a 24 by 32 inch box you begin to appreciate what can be planted in small space.

In the carrot-onion-radish box we sowed the carrots in 4 inch-wide bands spaced 5 inches apart. After thinning and eating baby carrots we had 2 rows of mature carrots in each band—a total of 66 carrots. The planting of onion sets yielded more than 50 green onions.

In the "salad box" we managed to get 4 heads of Bibb lettuce and 4 heads of leaf lettuce in addition to carrots and onions.

The ground rules for planting in bands and spacing between bands was followed in planting the 3 by 9-foot gardens. Add the two variations of the 3 by 9 plan to see what can be done in a 3 by 18-foot space garden. A trellis for cucumbers adds a crop without adding much ground space. Plants in tubs, boxes and 5 gallon cans are the planner's best friends when it comes to bringing the concentrated 3 by 9 garden up to meaningful production.

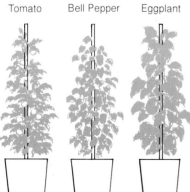

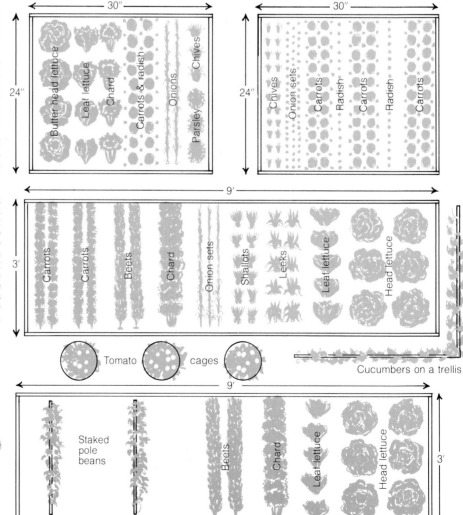

The no-soil-space garden. You can plan your balcony, deck, or patio garden in terms of boxes, tubs, bushel baskets, cans, and planters of all shapes and sizes.

One way to plan for a reasonable supply of vegetables from a container garden is illustrated below. Take a 24- by 30-inch box 6 inches deep as one basic unit, and a container 12 inches square as another. You also could use larger-sized units, but a smaller size is simply more portable.

The choice of vegetables. In choosing which vegetables to plant in your box garden, pick those you like best, of course—and of those, choose the ones that will yield the highest return per square foot of space—that is, the vegetables with the closest spacing in the row.

If you turn to the planting chart on page 56 and check the "Distance between plants" column, you'll find these vegetables in the close-spacing group: carrots, beets, chives, leaf lettuce, mustard, green onions, radishes, and turnips. Just check the planting distance for the vegetables you want to plant, and then you'll know how far apart to space the rows.

One way to get a continuous harvest is to plant a total of 6 boxes: 2 with vegetables that can take early planting; 2 more planted 3 weeks later; and 2 more 2 weeks later. How vegetables behave in your climate will dictate which ones to choose for late-spring and fall plantings. An advantage of box plantings is that you can think of your harvests in terms of the number of meals rather than in terms of total quantity.

But plants have tops that take up space. Therefore, you need to consider the distance between rows. If you look down the column "Distance between rows"

Here is a no-nonsense 25 by 30 foot garden planned to bring a succession of crops throughout the growing season. A block 10 feet wide and 30 feet long is set up for succession plantings starting with the early cool weather crops in the first 10 by 10 foot block. Second 10 by 10 block is for succession planting a month later. The 3rd block takes care of the crops that will mature in the fall. As space opens in the first block by harvesting early maturing crops, it also is planted for late fall maturing.

The warm season vegetables occupy the rest of the space. The corn is planted in 3 blocks of 3 rows in 3 plantings 2 weeks apart.

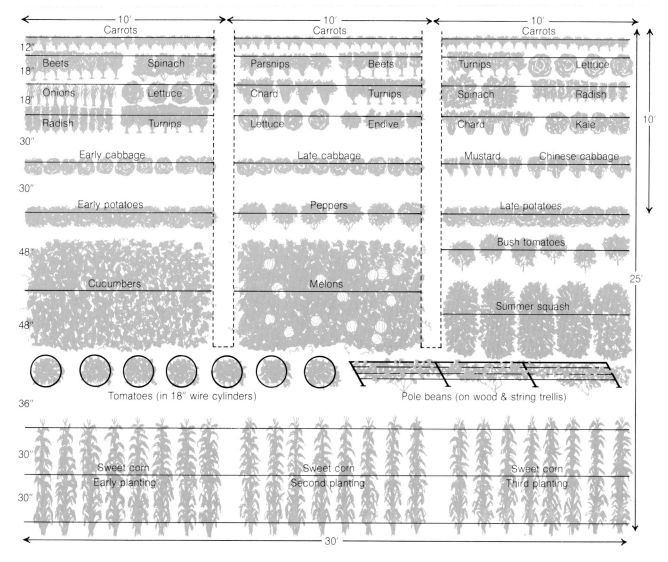

in the chart, you'll see that the shortest distance is 12 inches, and that most vegetables call for a distance of 18 inches. In the box garden, how much can you cheat on those distances?

Since you won't have to walk through the plants, and since you'll be using your fingers rather than a hoe to cultivate and weed, you shouldn't really need such distances as 12 to 18 inches.

But a vegetable does need normal head room in order to reach normal size. For example, if you crowd head lettuce much closer than 10 inches in the row, you will harvest 3 heads—but they will be poor ones, and all of them combined will give you no more lettuce than 2 good heads would. So consider head room, and allow 10 inches between the wide rows.

Charting Successions

When you chart a succession of plantings on paper, it makes the goal of a long harvest season seem easy to reach.

The starting dates in your garden may vary from the dates on the sample chart shown here, depending on your climate zone, but the idea of successive plantings is valid everywhere.

The small-space gardener has to find a place for the second or third planting; you can't plant lettuce on top of lettuce. One solution is *intercropping*—planting quick-maturing crops between slow growers. From their own experiences, our panel of gardeners offered these suggestions for successful successive plantings:

Plant lettuce transplants in the shade of bush snap beans.

Broadcast turnips between cabbages.

Tuck in green onion sets almost everywhere.

Thin lettuce, then transplant them for a later crop.

Grow radishes alongside almost any vegetable.

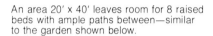

An area 20' x 40' leaves room for 8 raised beds with ample paths between—similar to the garden shown below.

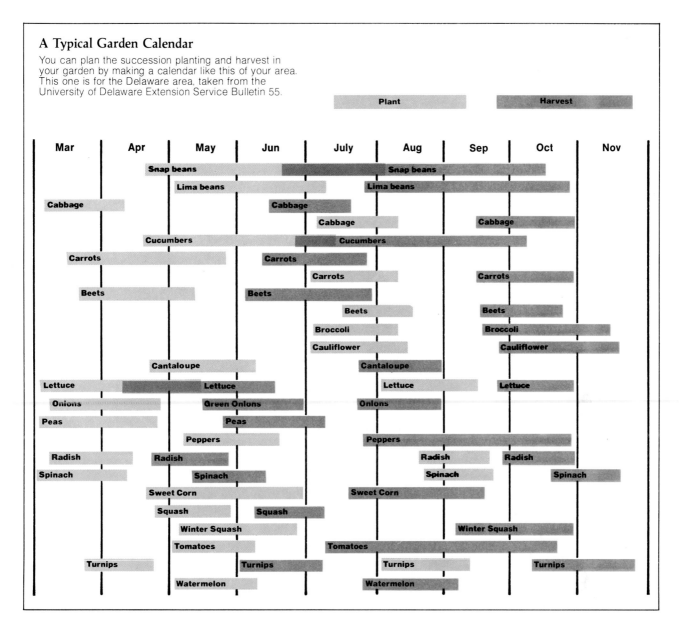

A Typical Garden Calendar

You can plan the succession planting and harvest in your garden by making a calendar like this of your area. This one is for the Delaware area, taken from the University of Delaware Extension Service Bulletin 55.

Plant   Harvest

Mar	Apr	May	Jun	July	Aug	Sep	Oct	Nov

Snap beans · Snap beans
Lima beans · Lima beans
Cabbage · Cabbage · Cabbage · Cabbage
Cucumbers · Cucumbers
Carrots · Carrots · Carrots · Carrots
Beets · Beets · Beets · Beets
Broccoli · Broccoli
Cauliflower · Cauliflower
Cantaloupe · Cantaloupe
Lettuce · Lettuce · Lettuce · Lettuce
Onions · Green Onions · Onions
Peas · Peas
Peppers · Peppers
Radish · Radish · Radish · Radish
Spinach · Spinach · Spinach · Spinach
Sweet Corn · Sweet Corn
Squash · Squash
Winter Squash · Winter Squash
Tomatoes · Tomatoes
Turnips · Turnips · Turnips · Turnips
Watermelon · Watermelon

The 3- by 9-foot garden. Whether your garden space is 3 by 9, 4 by 9, or 3 by 27, your planning problems will be about the same.

You will do the best job of planning of a 3- or 4-foot-wide garden if you visualize it as a series of planter boxes, similar to those illustrated. As the length increases, the variety of vegetables increases.

To get continuous harvests in such a small garden, keep stand-by plants growing in 4-inch pots, and be ready to pop them into the garden after you've harvested any crop.

The large small garden. The plan shown on page 45 for a no-nonsense 25 by 30 garden shows the succession of planting, from early season to late. The dates of planting each block will vary according to your climate. See the "When to plant" category for each specific vegetable.

If you have enough space, you could plant such space-requiring vegetables as vines of winter squash and melons. Corn would require wider blocks.

If you analyze the progression from a box garden to a 25- by 30- or 30- by 50-square-foot garden, you will find that the areas with the high concentration per square foot do not increase in proportion to size. For example, the 25 by 30 garden is the same as three 9 by 12 gardens planted in succession. The choice of vegetables and the number of each is a personal thing. The 25 by 30 plan in the photo on page 46 shows that this planner, for example, loves lettuce.

PLANTING AND CARE

This "nuts and bolts" chapter contains the necessary information for getting the plants started, in the ground, and protected from damage once they're planted.

You'd think that sowing seeds ¼ or ½ or 1 inch deep, covering them with soil, and keeping the soil damp would be a simple matter—but it isn't, nor is it always a successful one.

One of our gardeners confessed: "For the first time in 13 years absolute failures were experienced. Diseases not before experienced were seen. Plants in excellent health from my greenhouse grew magnificently and then perished. Corn, cabbage, butternut squash, and onions did not even appear from seed."

Every now and then, seeds just won't germinate. Even the best gardeners have experienced failure.

A first-time gardener can kill by kindness, so follow these suggestions: don't overdo the preparation of a seed bed. Don't rake the soil until it is fine as dust— that's the way to make mud pies. When the soil dries out after being watered, the seeds will be imprisoned in a tight crust of soil. Don't tenderly cover the seed with loose soil—seed must have contact with soil.

To firm the soil over the seed, pat it or tamp it with the side of a rake, the flat of a hoe, or a short piece of 2 by 4.

If your soil is uncooperative because of heavy clay, and you don't want to tackle the soil in the entire garden, add compost or other organic material just to the row you wish to plant.

Don't rush the season. With many seeds—for example, corn and beans (especially limas in cold soil)—there's a race between rooting and rotting. In this case, the warmer the soil, the better the chances for success.

If spring planting fever gets you while the soil is still cold, choose the plant whose seeds will tolerate cool soil. See the planting chart on page 56.

Depth of seed. The old rule of thumb is: plant at a depth equal to 4 times the diameter of the seed. But as with all rules, you must use your own judgment— even as far as the specific depth listed in the planting chart is concerned. So plant shallow in wet weather or in heavy soils, and plant deeper if soils are light and sandy and dry weather is anticipated.

Several crops benefit by very shallow planting, ¼ inch or less. These include parsnips, carrots, parsley, cress, and, to a lesser degree, lettuce.

But when you plant seeds with a long germination period so shallowly, you must pay close attention to sprinkling so that the soil surface never becomes dry.

To prevent drying out and crusting of soil surface, some gardeners cover soil rows with burlap sacks and sprinkle them with water, as necessary. With sacks, however, there is always the danger of forgetting them for a few days at emergence time.

A ⅛-inch mulch of vermiculite, bark, or sawdust will prevent crusting and reduce the required frequency of sprinkling. In windy weather it's a good idea to contain the mulch in a slot to prevent it from blowing away.

2

3

How to Install Plastic Mulches

5

6

These photos (from various university experiment stations) show a typical installation of black plastic mulch. **1.** Dig a shallow furrow or trench on each side of the row, approximately as wide as the plastic. **2.** Secure the end of the plastic at the end of the row. **3.** Roll out the plastic evenly along the row. Secure the plastic's edges by burying them in a trench and covering them with soil.

4. A "bulb-planter" is an excellent tool to cut plastic and dig small transplanting holes. (Sharpen the tool's edges with a file.) Or cut a cross-shaped slit in the plastic and manually dig a small hole (this alternative is as effective, but less fast). The size of the slit will depend on the size of the root ball you intend to plant.

5. Here, a finished planting hole awaits a transplant in a Jiffy 7 pellet. In hard soil, a small amount of soil substitute can be used in the hole to give the transplant's root system a good start.

6. Transplant as usual.

7. The look of the planted row. Water the trench on either side of the row. Side seepage irrigates the row.

8. Properly done, the results should look like this.

7

8

Clear plastic is a good mulch but you need to watch closely for the emergence of seedlings. Remove the plastic as soon as the seedlings show. Otherwise the rapid buildup of heat on a sunny day will burn the tender plants.

What makes a good mulch cover? Bernard Pollack of Rutgers answered the question this way: "I think plastic is the answer. Make a shallow trough and plant seeds at bottom—cover trough with plastic (clear only) at an angle so water can run off. (See illustration below.)

"In New Jersey we call this 'trench culture' and we have had exceptionally good results with direct seeding of hard-to-germinate seeds like tomato, pepper, eggplant. The plastic cover prevents evaporation; heats the soil 20 to 30° higher than air temperature; and makes the seed germinate fast. This prevents loss from disease. Clear plastic should be removed after germination so it is possible to control weeds that have also grown under the mulch."

"Scatter" sowing. Consider the advantages of sowing seeds of carrots, beets, and leaf lettuce in 3- or 4-inch-wide bands rather than in a single line row. For one thing, the problem of the first thinning is not as critical. With carrots, for example, there is less chance of tangled, malformed roots if the same number of seeds you normally sow in a foot of row are spaced out in a band 3 to 4 inches wide. You'll have to do some thinning, of course, but much of it will be in pulling baby carrots. The disadvantage of having a wide row, however, is that you have to hand weed.

Commercial carrot growers spread carrot seeds in a 6-inch band by equipping the planter with a "scatter shoe."

You can use this method of sowing for all fine-seeded vegetables that are used in the immature stage—for example, beets and turnips for green tops, and leaf lettuce and mustard for young leaves.

Spacing the seeds in the furrow. Some of the ways of dropping seed in the furrow appear below. Here are a few more.

Sow small seeds in groups of 2 to 6, leaving a few inches between groups. Supposedly, the seeds help each other up when the soil is likely to crust over, and help ensure against seed failures.

Mix small seeds and white sand in a saltshaker and shake the mix into the furrow so you can see where you've scattered the seeds.

If you like the spacing of your small seeds to be precise, try this: Spread single sheets of facial tissue in the seed furrow. The seeds will show up clearly against the white paper; you can move them easily with a pencil or toothpick. The tissue will rot away long before the seeds germinate.

Seed tape, available commercially, helps you sow fine seeds precisely—seeds spaced at exact distances are enclosed in water-soluble plastic.

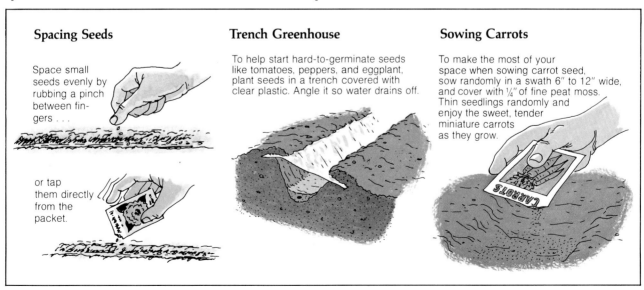

Spacing Seeds

Space small seeds evenly by rubbing a pinch between fingers . . .

or tap them directly from the packet.

Trench Greenhouse

To help start hard-to-germinate seeds like tomatoes, peppers, and eggplant, plant seeds in a trench covered with clear plastic. Angle it so water drains off.

Sowing Carrots

To make the most of your space when sowing carrot seed, sow randomly in a swath 6" to 12" wide, and cover with ¼" of fine peat moss. Thin seedlings randomly and enjoy the sweet, tender miniature carrots as they grow.

Tomato transplants should be stocky, not leggy; have 4-6 true leaves; and be young and succulent.

Weeds. The competition between vegetable seedlings and weed seedlings is always a problem. Every time you work the soil, you bring weed seeds up to the surface, where they find the best conditions for germination. And covering your plants with clear plastic or a mulch will aid the weeds as well as your crop.

First-time gardeners often wonder whether their packet of seeds wasn't ½ weed seeds. In fact, Gerald Burke of the Burpee Company says that it is a frequent protest: "One complaint we run into quite consistently is the story of the gardener who plants good seed out of the packet, but nothing but weeds come up. I guess this one bugs us as much as anything else. With today's highly developed techniques in cleaning vegetable and flower seed, the chance of weed seed appearing in any of these crops along with the good seed is negligible. There is 1,000 times more weed seed in the soil than is ever going to be in a packet of seed."

Transplants

Ordinarily, seed the root crops, beans, peas, corn, pumpkin, and squashes directly where you want them to grow. But tomatoes, peppers, and eggplants are almost always set out as transplants. Cabbage and its relatives, lettuce, onions, and melons can be started either way.

The most important reason for growing transplants is to save time. This method lets the plant grow before the frost danger is over and before the soil is dry enough to work. It actually lengthens the growing season by 1 to 2 months.

Starting from transplants avoids some of the hazards common to seedlings —birds, insects, heavy rain, and weeds.

Whether you buy transplants or grow your own depends on whether you can buy the varieties you want and how you feel about starting from scratch. If you enjoy it, do it.

Different gardeners have different methods of growing from seed to transplant size. Some of the ways the gardeners on our panel handled the job are illustrated opposite.

Success in growing good transplants depends on these basic requirements:
1. A disease-free growing medium.
2. Warmth and moisture for seed germination.
3. Adequate light for stocky growth.
4. An adjustment period to ready the indoor plant to be in open outdoor conditions.

These requirements can be met in several different ways.

Soil for seeds. Start the seed in a medium that is free from disease-causing organisms.

You can buy excellent germinating and growing materials and plant containers at garden supply centers.

Vermiculite. A lightweight expanded mica.

Synthetic soil mix. Jiffy Mix, Pro-Mix, and Redi-Earth are examples. Seeds are sown in it, and the seedlings grow in it.

Jiffy-7 pellets. A compressed peat pellet containing fertilizer. When placed in water it expands to make a 1¾- by 2-inch container. After it expands, place the seed directly in the container.

BR8 blocks. A plant-growing fiber block containing fertilizer. Water the block thoroughly and place the seed directly in the block.

Kys-Kube. A ready-to-use fiber cube containing fertilizer. Water the cube thoroughly, then place the seeds directly in it.

Fiber pots—trays—strips. Containers made of peat or other fibrous material. Fill with synthetic soil mix for growing seedlings in. Since the container and plant are set out right into the garden soil, there is no root disturbance.

Plastic. Pots or trays in various sizes and shapes. They must have drain holes in the bottom. Fill with synthetic soil mix for growing seedlings. Tip out the root ball when transplanting.

Starting Seeds

Here are some good ideas for starting seed and handling transplants that we picked up from creative backyard gardeners:

Wire wickets to hold plastic up

Ventilation holes

Seeds planted in a nursery flat. A large plastic bag around the flat seals in moisture and heat for quick germination

The plastic bag works around a tray of pots, too

Cottage cheese or margarine tubs make great seed-starting containers

Propagating mat or heating cables keep containers or flats at the proper temperature

Cut a plastic jug—plant in the bottom section. Use the top for protection when it's needed.

Cut-off milk cartons make excellent transplant containers: perforate around the bottom for easy removal when transplanting time comes.

Transplanting

1. Ready the plant. If it's in a peat pot, tear the top edge off so it can't act as a wick and dry out the root ball.
2. If it's in a plastic, fiber, or clay pot, tip it out—don't pull it out by the stem.
3. After planting, firm the soil around the transplant. Then water lightly to settle the soil and remove any air pockets that may be left around the root ball.
4. To make sure the root ball stays moist during the first few critical days, build a small temporary basin, a little larger than the root system.

Seed Starting Containers

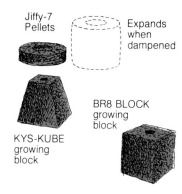

Jiffy-7 Pellets

Expands when dampened

KYS-KUBE growing block

BR8 BLOCK growing block

One-step method

Sow seeds, 2 at a time, directly into plastic pots, peat pots, Kys-cubes, BR8 blocks, Jiffy-7 pellets. Water thoroughly and place on a tray in a plastic bag. They'll be ready to transplant when about 6 inches high.

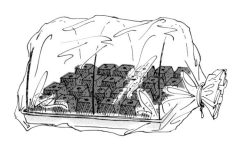

Seeds In Vermiculite

Sow seeds about ¼- to ½-inch deep in the moistened vermiculite. Pat lightly to firm the vermiculite around the seeds. Water lightly and cover with paper, or slip the seed tray into a plastic bag.

When the first true leaves of the seedlings have formed, dig them out carefully and transplant them into peat pots, plastic pots, or some kind of container that's filled with the synthetic soil. Make a small hole in the mix in the container and set the seedling in this hole so that the seed leaves are ½ inch from the surface. Press the mix firmly around the roots and stem. Water carefully. One advantage in starting seeds in vermiculite is that it is easy to lift out the seedlings without damaging the roots.

When you use vermiculite as the seeding "soil" and the mix of peat moss and vermiculite as the seedling "soil," you protect the seedlings from disease organisms common in garden soil and composts that often cause the seedlings to "damp off" and die.

If you wish to use compost or garden soil or to add either to the mix, it's a good idea to sterilize them.

You can sterilize small quantities by baking the soil in the oven. Some experienced gardeners put the soil in coffee cans and bake at 350° for 1½ hours. Others place a potato in the soil before baking, and consider it sterilized when the potato is done. If shallow containers are used, the timing may be shortened. As soon as *all* the soil reaches 180°, the job is done. In a shallow pan, the soil may reach that temperature in 45 minutes with the oven at 350°. Overcooking can release toxic substances in the soil, so keep a close watch.

Seeds In Blocks Or Cubes

Sow the seed directly in the small blocks and in the expanding Jiffy-7s—but moisten the material thoroughly before you sow the seeds. Put them in the warmest spot you can find. To germinate quickly, tomato, eggplant, and pepper seeds need a soil temperature of 75° to 85°.

Cover the blocks with paper or slip them into a plastic bag to prevent them from drying out. Then you shouldn't have to water until the seeds have sprouted.

When the seedlings emerge, keep them in full sunlight—12 hours a day, if possible. The temperatures for seedling growth should be between 70° to 75° during the day and 60° to 65° during the night.

Setting Out

Set transplants into the soil carefully, causing as little root disturbance as possible. Peat pots, cubes, and blocks will cause very little root disturbance, but be sure that all such containers are below soil level to prevent the root ball from drying out rapidly.

It helps to pack the soil down around the root ball. It also helps to "spot" water the root ball in addition to providing regular irrigation. You'll be able to tip out plants in plastic or clay pots more easily if the soil is wet.

If a plant is growing in a light soil mix, don't set it in a small hole in heavy soil. Instead, blend organic matter in a larger planting hole so that there is no abrupt change in soil texture.

See "Experienced Advice," page 68, for ways to protect transplants.

12 Hours Of Sunlight

If you're growing transplants indoors, it's easy enough to get directions for the ideal way to grow them—and the directions are easy to follow if "indoors" is a fully equiped greenhouse. But if you can't find a spot with 12 hours of sunlight and temperatures that fluctuate from 70° days and 65° nights throughout the growing period, what do you do? The answer is: you make do. Our panel gardeners carried out the transplant procedure in many ways, some of which appear below.

Below: A 4' x 8' clear fiberglass panel is arched over part of a row at sunset each day and removed the next morning. Soil and air temperatures read at 11 p.m. were higher than those in the open row. Plastic-covered peppers grew faster and larger than those in open ground.

"Hardening" Transplants

Young plants should not go directly from an indoor environment to the open garden. Instead, take them outside in the daytime and bring them in again at night if frost is likely. In one way or another, expose them to lower temperatures about 2 weeks before you set them out. Also, gradually expose them to more sunlight.

Protecting the transplants with hot caps or plastic covers in early plantings has more advantages than warming the soil and protecting them from frost.

It is equally important to protect the young plants from being ripped about by winds.

When using hot caps or plastic covers, be sure there's some ventilation so that the young plants are not cooked by the heat buildup.

How To Use The Planting Chart

"Depth to plant seed." A quick look at the fractions tells you that many gardeners plant too deep.

"Number of seed to sow per foot." The figures provide one answer to the question, "How thick or thin should I sow the seeds?" Our figures give the average of 6 expert seed-sowers—3 pessimists and 3 optimists.

"Distance between plants." The first figure is the minimum. You get better growth with wider spacing—it cuts down on the competition.

"Distance between rows." The minimum distance assumes that space is limited and weeding will be done with hand tools. Wider distance between rows is preferable and power equipment is used, if necessary.

"Number of days to germination." The number of days varies with the soil temperature. Early spring sowings will take longer than later plantings. The range is given in answer to questions like, "How long do I wait before I know I have to reseed?"

1. A small, hinged A-frame increases spring soil temperatures. Open ends allow circulation. It easily can be picked up and stored when not needed.
2. Shingles stuck in the ground help protect young tomato transplants.
3. In commercial plantings in San Diego County, California, clear plastic is used for windbreaks, soil mulch, and row cover, as the site and season demand.
4. Gallon-size bottomless plastic jugs are useful protectors for tender plants. Be sure to leave the cap off to provide ventilation.

"Soil temperature for seed." Seeds that "need cool soil" do best in a temperature range of 50° to 65°; those that "tolerate cool soil" prefer a 50° to 85° range; those that "need warm soil" excel in a 65° to 85° range.

"Weeks needed to grow to transplant size." The variation of 4 to 6, 5 to 7, and 10 to 12 weeks allows for hot-bed-greenhouse, window-sill, and under-grow-lamp conditions. Generally, the warmer the growing conditions, the shorter the time needed to grow transplants. However, allowance must be made for a change from an indoor to an outdoor environment. See page 55.

"Days to maturity." The figures in this column show the *relative* length of time it takes to grow a crop from seed or transplant to table use. The time will vary with variety and season.

Vegetable	Depth to plant seed (inches)	Number of seed to sow per foot	Distance between plants (inches)	Distance between rows (inches)	Number of days to germination	Soil temperature for seed			Weeks needed to grow to transplant size	Days to maturity	Remarks
						Needs cool soil	Tolerates cool soil	Needs warm soil			
Artichoke	½		60	72	7-14		•		4-6	12 mos	Start with divisions preferred.
Asparagus	1½		18	36	7-21		•		1 year	3 years	Sow in spring and transplant the following spring.
Beans: Snap Bush	1½-2	6-8	2-3	18-30	6-14			•		45-65	Make sequence plantings.
Snap Pole	1½-2	4-6	4-6	36-48	6-14			•		60-70	Long bearing season if kept picked.
Lima Bush	1½-2	5-8	3-6	24-30	7-12		•	•		60-80	Needs warmer soil than snap beans.
Lima Pole	1½-2	4-5	6-10	30-36	7-12			•		85-90	
Fava—Broadbean Winsor Bean	2½	5-8	3-4	18-24	7-14		•			80-90	Hardier than the common bean.
Garbanzo— Chick Pea	1½-2	5-8	3-4	24-30	6-12			•		105	
Scarlet Runner	1½-2	4-6	4-6	36-48	6-14			•		60-70	Will grow in cooler summers than common beans.
Soybean	1½-2	6-8	2-3	24-30	6-14			•		55-85 95-100	Choose varieties to fit your climate. See text.
Beets	½-1	10-15	2	12-18	7-10		•			55-65	Thin out extra plants and use for greens.
Black-eye Cowpea Southern Peas	½-1	5-8	3-4	24-30	7-10			•		65-80	
Yardlong Bean Asparagus Bean	½-1	2-4	12-24	24-36	6-13			•		65-80	Variety of Black eye peas. Grow as pole bean.
Broccoli, sprouting	½	10-15	14-18	24-30	3-10		•		5-7*	60-80T	80-100 days from seed.
Brussels Sprouts	½	10-15	12-18	24-30	3-10		•		4-6*	80-90T	100-110 days from seed.
Cabbage	½	8-10	12-20	24-30	4-10		•		5-7*	65-95T	Use thinnings for transplants. 90-150 days from seed.
Cabbage, Chinese	½	8-16	10-12	18-24	4-10		•		4-6	80-90	Best as seeded fall crop.
Cardoon	½	4-6	18	36	8-14		•		8	120-150	Transplanting to harvest about 90 days.
Carrot	¼	15-20	1-2	14-24	10-17		•			60-80	Start using when ½" in diameter to thin stand.
Cauliflower	½	8-10	18	30-36	4-10		•		5-7*	55-65T	70-120 days from seed.
Celeriac	⅛	8-12	8	24-30	9-21	•			10-12*	90-120T	Keep seeds moist.
Celery	⅛	8-12	8	24-30	9-21	•			10-12*	90-120T	Keep seeds moist.
Celtuce— Asparagus Lettuce	½	8-10	12	18	4-10		•		4-6	80	Same culture as lettuce.
Chard, Swiss	1	6-10	4-8	18-24	7-10		•			55-65	Use thinnings for early greens.
Chicory—Witloof (Belgian Endive)	¼	8-10	4-8	18-24	5-12		•			90-120	Force mature root for Belgian Endive.
Chives	½	8-10	8	10-16	8-12		•			80-90	Also propagate by division of clumps.
Collards	¼	10-12	10-15	24-30	4-10		•		4-6*	65-85T	Direct seed for a fall crop.
Corn, Sweet	2	4-6	10-14	30-36	6-10			•		60-90	Make successive plantings.
Corn Salad	½	8-10	4-6	12-16	7-10		•			45-55	Tolerant of cold weather.
Cress, Garden	¼	10-12	2-3	12-16	4-10		•			25-45	Seeds sensitive to light.
Cucumber	1	3-5	12	48-72	6-10			•	4	55-65	See text about training.
Dandelion	½	6-10	8-10	12-16	7-14		•			70-90	
Eggplant	¼-½	8-12	18	36	7-14			•	6-9*	75-95T	

*Transplants preferred over seed.
T Number of days from setting out transplants; all others are from seeding.

Vegetable	Depth to plant seed (inches)	Number of seed to sow per foot	Distance between plants (inches)	Distance between rows (inches)	Number of days to germination	Soil temperature for seed			Weeks needed to grow to transplant size	Days to maturity	Remarks
						Needs cool soil	Tolerates cool soil	Needs warm soil			
Endive	½	4-6	9-12	12-24	5-9		•		4-6	60-90	Same culture as lettuce.
Wonder Berry Garden Huckleberry	½	8-12	24-36	24-36	5-15			•	5-10	60-80	
Fennel, Florence	½	8-12	6	18-24	6-17		•			120	Plant in fall in mild winter areas.
Garlic	1		2-4	12-18	6-10		•			90-sets	
Ground Cherry Husk Tomato	½	6	24	36	6-13			•	6*	90-100T	Treat same as tomatoes.
Horseradish	Div.		10-18	24			•			6-8 mth.	Use root division 2-8" long.
Jerusalem Artichoke	Tubers 4		15-24	30-60			•			100-105	
Kale	½	8-12	8-12	18-24	3-10		•		4-6	55-80	Direct seed for fall crop.
Kohlrabi	½	8-12	3-4	18-24	3-10		•		4-6	60-70	
Leeks	½-1	8-12	2-4	12-18	7-12		•		10-12	80-90T	130-150 days from seed.
Lettuce: Head	¼-½	4-8	12-14	18-24	4-10	•			3-5	55-80	Keep seed moist.
Leaf	¼-½	8-12	4-6	12-18	4-10	•			3-5	45-60	Keep seed moist.
Muskmelon	1	3-6	12	48-72	4-8			•	3-4	75-100	
Mustard	½	8-10	2-6	12-18	3-10		•			40-60	Use early to thin.
Nasturtium	½-1	4-8	4-10	18-36			•			50-60	
Okra	1	6-8	15-18	28-36	7-14			•		50-60	
Onion: sets	1-2		2-3	12-24		•				95-120	Green onions 50-60 days.
plants	2-3		2-3	12-24		•			8	95-120T	
seed	½	10-15	2-3	12-24	7-12	•				100-165	
Parsley	¼-½	10-15	3-6	12-20	14-28		•		8	85-90	
Parsnips	½	8-12	3-4	16-24	15-25		•			100-120	
Peas	2	6-7	2-3	18-30	6-15	•				65-85	
Peanut	1½	2-3	6-10	30				•		110-120	Requires warm growing season.
Peppers	¼	6-8	18-24	24-36	10-20			•	6-8	60-80T	
Potato	4	1	12	24-36	8-16		•			90-105	
Pumpkin	1-1½	2	30	72-120	6-10			•		70-110	Give them room.
Purslane	½	6-8	6	12	7-14		•				
Radish	½	14-16	1-2	6-12	3-10	•				20-50	Early spring or late fall weather.
Rhubarb	Crown		36	60			•				Matures 2nd season.
Rocket	¼	8-10	8-12	18-24	7-14	•					
Rutabaga	½	4-6	8-12	18-24	3-10		•			80-90	
Salsify	½	8-12	2-3	16-18		•				110-150	
Salsify, Black	½	8-12	2-3	16-18		•				110-150	
Shallot	Bulb—1		2-4	12-18			•			60-75	
Spinach	½	10-12	2-4	12-14	6-14	•				40-65	
Malabar	½	4-6	12	12	10		•			70	
New Zealand	1½	4-6	18	24	5-10		•			70-80	
Tampala	¼-½	6-10	4-6	24-30			•			21-42	Thin and use early while tender.
Squash (summer)	1	4-6	16-24	36-60	3-12			•		50-60	
Squash (winter)	1	1-2	24-48	72-120	6-10			•		85-120	
Sunflower	1	2-3	16-24	36-48	7-12			•		80-90	Space wide for large heads.
Sweet Potato	Plants		12-18	36-48				•		120	Propagate from cuttings.
Tomato	½		18-36	36-60	6-14			•	5-7	55-90T	Early var. 55-60. Mid 65-75, Late 80-100.
Turnip	½	14-16	1-3	15-18	3-10	•				45-60	Thin early for greens.
Watermelon	1		12-16	60	3-12			•		80-100	Ice-box size mature earlier.

*Transplants preferred over seed.
T Number of days from setting out transplants; all others are from seeding.

Pests and Controls

Aphids

Aphids
Crop affected: Especially cabbage, cauliflower, Brussels sprouts, and broccoli. The aphid is a general feeder.
How to control: Spray with Malathion.

Leafhoppers

Leafhoppers
Crop affected: Lettuce, potatoes, beans, carrots, celery; general feeder.
How to control: Most frequent controls are Malathion or Sevin. Leafhoppers are piercing and sucking insects that may need weekly applications for control. They feed on blossoms of beans and cause a poor pod set.

White Flies

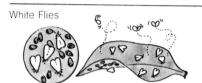

White Flies
Crop affected: Tomatoes, beans, and many more.
How to control: Get at them at the first sign. Nymphs do most of the damage. Use Malathion, making sure to cover the underside of leaves thoroughly. You may need to spray 4 times at weekly intervals to clean them out.

Cabbage Looper

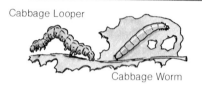

Cabbage Worm

Cabbage Looper, Cabbage Worm
Crop affected: Broccoli, Brussels sprouts, cabbage, and cauliflower.
How to control: Spray or dust on appearance, and apply weekly, as needed. The first choice is Sevin. Start using *Bacillus thuringiensis* (Dipel, Biotrol Thuricide) when worms are small; worms must ingest the material. Very safe.

Colorado Potato Beetle

Bean Leaf Beetle

Mexican Bean Beetle

Colorado Potato Beetle, Mexican Bean Beetle, Bean Leaf Beetle
Crop affected: Beans, peppers, and eggplant.
How to control: Same controls as for cucumber beetles. Young plants of eggplant are vulnerable to potato beetle attack. Look for damage when the first leaves unfold.

Cucumber Beetles,

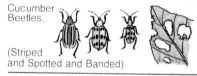

(Striped and Spotted and Banded)

Cucumber Beetles (Striped and Spotted and Banded)
Crop affected: Cucumbers, squash, melons, and pumpkins.
How to control: Spray or dust when beetles appear, and weekly, as needed. Use Sevin dust or spray, Methoxychior, or Diazinon.

Flea Beetle

Blister Beetle

Flea Beetle, Blister Beetle
Crop affected: Peppers, potatoes, and tomatoes.
How to control: Spray or dust when the damage first is noticed. Use the same controls as for cucumber beetles.

Cutworm

Cutworm
Crop affected: At night, the cutworm cuts off small plants at soil level. Tomatoes, cabbage, peppers, beans, and corn may be destroyed.
How to control: Dust or spray in a band along the row with Sevin. Or control before planting with a soil application of Diazinon granules or dust. This will also stop wire worm damage. See label.

Squash Vine Borer

Squash Bug

Squash Vine Borer, Squash Bug
Crop affected: Cucumbers, melons, pumpkins, and squash.
How to control: Look for appearance after June 15. Dust with Sevin to get nymphs. Apply 3 times at 10-day intervals.

Corn Borer

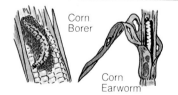

Corn Earworm

Corn Earworm, Corn Borer
Crop affected: Corn.
How to control: The first generation shows up in June and July; the second generation in August. Dust foliage with Sevin for corn borers. For corn earworms, dust silks when they emerge, and repeat every 2 to 3 days until silks turn brown.

The Spoilers

One of the questionnaires we used with gardeners throughout the United States included these questions:

"What disappointments did you have in last year's garden? Crop failure? Mistakes? Why?—or where do you think you went wrong?"

"What success did you have?"

"Did anything surprise you? We are interested in both good and bad surprises—as well as what caused them, if you know."

Replies came from gardeners of all beliefs about the use of insecticides and fungicides. Several had tried getting by without paying any attention to insects and diseases. The few answers that follow are typical of many and will give you an idea of the pleasures as well as the problems in gardening all over the country. Note that not all the spoilers were insects or diseases.

From Massachusetts
Failure: "We had a great deal of rain and cold weather during May. Quite a few different kinds of seeds didn't come up and had to be replanted. The bugs ate the plants as fast as they came up."
Success: "The cucumbers and pole beans and corn are going good now after the second planting."

From New Jersey
Failure: "I watered and weeded and felt we would have good vegetables but we were disappointed. Worms in the radishes. Tomatoes not so good."
(In answer to the question: "What varieties did you buy?" the answer was, "Don't remember, went mostly by the pictures.")

From New York
Failure: "Trouble with fusarium wilt on tomatoes, and corn borer and corn earworm."
Success: "Insect control other than corn. I tried to stick to a 10- to 14-day schedule through the growing season."

Did anything surprise you? "Results from succession of plantings; replanting of areas already planted."
"The amount of produce you can obtain from a 10- by 20-foot garden."
"How much better my garden looked than the organic garden next door."
Mistakes beginners make: "Using grass clippings from a lawn that has been treated with 2-4, D weed killer."

From Louisiana
Failures: "None to speak of."
Success: "Produced 27 vegetables—over $900 (at retail) worth on a 45- by 60-foot garden."

Did anything surprise you? "Marvel at nature's way of producing vegetables with a little help from the gardener."
Mistakes beginners make: "Plant too thick. Wrong varieties. Poor insect and disease control. Poor drainage. Lack of irrigation."

From Michigan
Failure: "All of first sweet pepper blossoms set and a good later crop resulted. About half of my potato seed rotted in the ground. I think I planted too early when the ground was wet."
Success: "The garden was a great success. Picked 150 cantaloupes. Picked over 4 bushels of tomatoes from 12 plants."

From Michigan
Failure: "All of my cauliflower, most broccoli, all cabbage plants were in-

All gardeners will agree on one point: nothing can compare with that "fresh from the garden" flavor.

Top: Long-time gardeners know their plot of ground—the characteristics of the soil, how much to water, when to get the soil ready for planting, and what fertilizer to use. Some of the most valuable gardening knowledge is based on experience.

Above: Raised beds frame a "show-off" planting of various kinds of lettuce. Leeks are in the foreground.

fected with root maggots, and as a result bolted and formed very small heads. My lettuce, endive, and escarole was riddled by larvae."

Success: "In my 50' by 50' garden I raised 3000 lbs. of table-ready vegetables, most of which my wife canned or froze."

From Ohio

Failure: "Didn't pick cabbage in time—heads split open. Didn't spray soon enough for cabbage worms. Though trained on stakes, many of the tomatoes touched the ground where they either rotted or were riddled with slugs."

Success: "Second planting of cucumbers a great success. Planted them alongside an arborvitae hedge upon which they climbed. Had a fine bean crop. A few bean plants had bacterial blight, but these I destroyed as soon as there was evidence of the disease."

From South Carolina

Failure: "Had a great deal of trouble with okra—mainly due to cold, wet weather. Eggplant got eaten up by flea beetles—that was my own fault for neglecting them."

Success: "This is the first year I have successfully grown melons, due I think to mulching and picking disease-resistant varieties."

From Indiana

Failure: "Baby Limas. Very little production late in the season probably due to small insects. Cucumbers—lost all plants either to wilt or insects."

Success: "Followed early plantings with late plantings. 'Double cropped' peas and beans, and peas and corn. Excellent beans, tomatoes, beets, broccoli, corn, cucumbers, peppers, spinach, carrots, and flowers."

Surprises: "How much we saved on groceries after September 1st."

From Southern California

Failure: "Summer crop was pretty much a failure. Tomatoes suffered from wilt and failure to set fruit. Green peppers and eggplant not good. Bush beans started out well, then turned yellow and died. Failure attributed to too much horse manure, too much water, too many insects, too many gophers."

Success: "The results with zucchini and Swiss chard were excellent. The winter crop of beets, cabbage, broccoli, radishes, lettuce and turnips were excellent."

County Agricultural Agent

After reading a hundred or so reports on successes and failures in the garden, we realized that we could not solve all the insect and disease problems. Check your County Agricultural Agent for special problems in your area.

You can get the 50-page booklet, *Insects and Diseases of Vegetables in the Home Garden*, for 30¢ by writing to the Superintendent of Documents, Government Printing Office, Washington D.C. 20402.

The chart on the previous page offers ways of controlling the most common insects. Root maggots are not listed, however. As many of our gardeners testified, these insects are disastrous on cabbage, all cabbage relatives, and radishes.

To stop the cabbage maggot from drilling holes in radishes, turnips, and rutabagas, either dust or sprinkle Diazinon over the seeded row after seeding. This mild treatment will kill the maggots as they hatch.

The same maggots bore into the stems of cabbage, cauliflower, and broccoli. The damage is more severe in spring plantings than in fall ones. To prevent this, make a solution of liquid Diazinon and pour a cupful around the stem of the transplants when you set them out.

When using insecticides on vegetables, check the label to find out how many days before the harvest you should stop spraying. They differ according to the insecticide and the vegetable. Since it's hard to treat each vegetable separately in a small, mixed-plant garden, stop spraying or dusting at least 2 weeks before the first harvest.

Choose Resistant Varieties

Planting disease-resistant varieties is the very best way to avoid crop failure due to diseases. The number of varieties bred for resistance to diseases is increasing every year. In the text, we have noted those varieties of each susceptible vegetable that has some disease resistance.

If you already have had trouble with diseases or want to avoid trouble in the future, check the variety list of these vegetables, both here and in catalogs, and look for mention of resistance to the diseases that damage the following vegetables:

Tomatoes—Fusarium, verticillium
Cucumbers—Scab, mosaic, downy mildew, powdery mildew, anathracnose
Muskmelon—Fusarium, powdery mildew
Snap beans—Mosaic, powdery mildew, root rot
Cabbage—Virus Yellows
Spinach—Blight, blue mold, downy mildew, mosaic

Our consultant, Raymond Sheldrake of Cornell, emphasizes the importance of resistant varieties:

"So many people tell me that their cucumber vines just up and die, even though they sprayed them. Well, the big problem is that their plants become infected with mosaic, a virus disease known as cucumber mosaic virus. The only way to escape it is to use mosaic-resistant varieties.

"In my radio programs I stress, for example, mosaic resistance in cucumbers and suggest mosaic-resistant varieties, but when someone who heard the program would go to a garden store, all they might find is a pretty picture of a cucumber on the outside of a seed packet. The variety might be 'Straight 8' with no resistance to anything, but the picture on the front of the package is what sells it. It's an open-pollinated cheap seed. Education is a slow process and I think we are closing the gap between what our breeders are doing and what our gardeners are using, mainly because some of these diseases have become so severe that the gardener just can't get by with any old variety."

Rotation

Controlling diseases by rotating crops is good and often-repeated advice in all garden literature. Rotation is most effective when you change the garden site every few years. Rotating crops within the garden so that the same crop does not occupy the same space year after year also will help some. (See the rotation plan in "Experienced Advice," page 72). But in the small 10- by 20-foot garden, rotation is difficult.

The Habit Of Cleanliness

The garden that is always clean and neat suffers less damage from diseases than a sloppy one. After you have harvested a crop, clean up all the vines, leaves, and fruit and spread them on the compost pile or spade them under it. In this way, you'll never have a weed over 2 weeks old. In a really clean garden, an infected plant stands out and you can destroy it quickly. Once you've got the habit of cleanliness, only a "clean plant" will be a healthy plant—and you'll water and fertilize to make it so.

All successful gardens, no matter how diverse in location, style, or size, have one thing in common: their owners follow the same basic good garden practices. These practices have been proven from one season to the next for as long as there have been gardens.

SMALL SPACE GARDENING

If you don't have a luxurious amount of rich, loamy soil, you can still find ways to grow vegetables in very limited spaces—and in doing so you can find ways to grow vegetables more effectively.

Perhaps you may have soil that won't support a vegetable garden. It may have a shallow layer of rocks or hardpan, or slow-draining heavy clay, or some other combination that is unfriendly to plants and hard to manage.

For such situations, the best solution is to grow plants above the soil. Raise the soil above ground level and keep it in place with 1" or 2" boards, with railroad ties (page 66), or brick or concrete.

If you can reach the raised bed from both sides, a width of 6' to 8' is practical. After all, you can plant, weed, and harvest without walking in the bed. If the raised bed is alongside a fence or for any reason accessible from only one side, make it 3' to 4' wide. The height of the bed should be at least 12" above the soil. If you build it 16" high and cap it with 2" x 6" boards, you can sit while you weed.

Fill this bed with a lightweight mix rich in organic matter to create a very efficient vegetable-growing factory. This will help water drain well through the soil and away from the bed. Unless the soil around the bed is flooded, the soil and the raised bed will never be waterlogged.

During a wet cool spring, the soil in the raised bed will warm up and be ready for planting weeks before regular garden soils can be seeded.

A well-built raised bed can support a lot of extras. You can use side boards to hold wire frames that keep out birds and rabbits or plastic covers to increase warmth or protect from frost. Plastic covers will prolong the growth of lettuce and other salad makings well into the winter.

There is another advantage to the raised bed that is seldom appreciated. Since it is a clean and neat structure, you will be more likely to keep it clean than you would an equal amount of planting space in a corner of the garden. Since weeds are more distracting in a raised bed, you will probably pull them more diligently than you would in a ground-level plot.

We may be prejudiced in favor of raised beds, but we are not alone. Others have endorsed this method, too (see "Carrots", page 84 and "Experienced Advice", page 70).

Vegetable factory. When you have limited space, you can afford to take measures that increase production and remove some of the hazards of conventional vegetable gardening. With a bit of ingenuity, you can rediscover the advantages of the old frame garden, the raised bed, the cold frame, and the hot bed.

In recent years many gardeners have taken the extra time and gone to the additional expense of installing raised beds. It's a sure way to ensure success.

Call it what you want to, it illustrates one way to concentrate the growing of vegetables in an environment that is free of any open-space gardening hazards. Using such a structure will add weeks to the growing season, both early and late. A choice of frames and covers can help avert damage caused by heavy rains and blistering sun during a heat wave. Use plastic covers when it rains, and lath or shade cloth when the summer sun is blazing hot. When wind damage is critical, use wire coverings.

When space is limited, gardening ingenuity crops up. Above: A specially constructed wooden planter houses cherry tomatoes and allysum. Above right: Containers, raised beds, and vertical plantings all make the most of this small space.

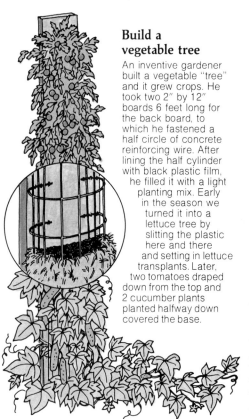

Build a vegetable tree

An inventive gardener built a vegetable "tree" and it grew crops. He took two 2" by 12" boards 6 feet long for the back board, to which he fastened a half circle of concrete reinforcing wire. After lining the half cylinder with black plastic film, he filled it with a light planting mix. Early in the season we turned it into a lettuce tree by slitting the plastic here and there and setting in lettuce transplants. Later, two tomatoes draped down from the top and 2 cucumber plants planted halfway down covered the base.

Vegetables In Containers

You can grow vegetables even when your garden is a balcony on the third floor of an apartment house, the patio of a mobile home, or a deck on a hillside or a roof top.

If you use one of the lightweight synthetic soils available at garden stores (see page 36), you can plant vegetables in boxes, baskets, plastic bags, clay pots, plastic pots, half-barrels, and wire cages to create the ideal environment for root growth.

Free of infested soil problems, tomatoes thrive so well in containers that even gardeners who have plenty of ground space are switching to pots, boxes, and baskets (see "Tomatoes," page 133).

You can plant eggplants and peppers instead of ornamentals on terraces and patios. A planter box 8" deep, 12" wide, and 3' long will deliver enough beets or carrots or lettuce for many meals.

The dirt gardener, with all the growing space desired, may laugh at the extreme measures some people will take to grow a few vegetables. But as the illustrations at right reveal, there is method in the madness.

When you're dealing with a waist-high planting space, weeding changes from a chore to play. These planting beds invite frequent attention.

Grass and tree roots can't invade the above-ground garden. And when your garden is above ground and portable, you can help it get as much sun as it needs.

Planting beds that fit into a level area gracefully or playfully invite the putterer, amaze the visitor, and prove that gardening doesn't have to be all that serious.

Vegetables grow up and hang down. As a small-space gardener, you can take full advantage of vertical space. Suddenly, a fence 5' high and 20' long becomes 100 square feet of gardening space. You can cover it with vines of beans, cucumbers, tomatoes, squash, or gourds without losing very much ground space. You can attach planter boxes to the fence for draping plants such as cherry tomatoes, pear tomatoes, the miniatures 'Tiny Tim' or 'Small Fry' tomatoes, or cucumbers. However, you must compensate for the limited soil space when you grow vegetables in planter boxes, on fences, or at the base of the fence. The more the roots are restricted, the more frequently you must water and add nutrients.

If you have only a limited space, you cannot overplant or waste the harvest, as occurs commonly in the conventional garden. Instead of trying to guess what a 20' row of beets will produce, you can sow seeds—a box or two of each, with the thinnings for greens—and harvest only what the cook calls for.

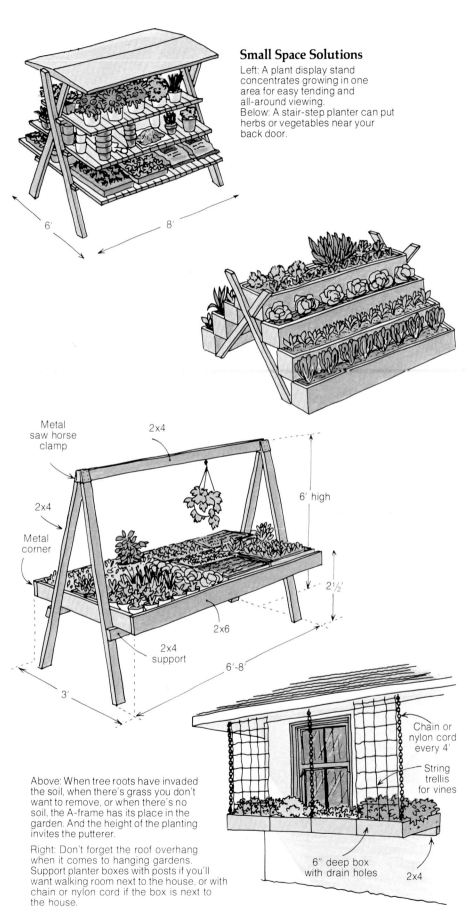

Small Space Solutions

Left: A plant display stand concentrates growing in one area for easy tending and all-around viewing.
Below: A stair-step planter can put herbs or vegetables near your back door.

6'

8'

Metal saw horse clamp

2x4

2x4

Metal corner

6' high

2½'

2x6

2x4 support

6'-8'

3'

Above: When tree roots have invaded the soil, when there's grass you don't want to remove, or when there's no soil, the A-frame has its place in the garden. And the height of the planting invites the putterer.

Right: Don't forget the roof overhang when it comes to hanging gardens. Support planter boxes with posts if you'll want walking room next to the house, or with chain or nylon cord if the box is next to the house.

Chain or nylon cord every 4'

String trellis for vines

6" deep box with drain holes

2x4

Tomatoes luxuriate in half a whiskey barrel, with 3 stakes for support.

Trellis training is one of the easiest methods. Here, a pot-grown plant was trained after the plant developed.

'Small Fry' in a planter box tied to a vertical frame made of 1" x 2" lumber.

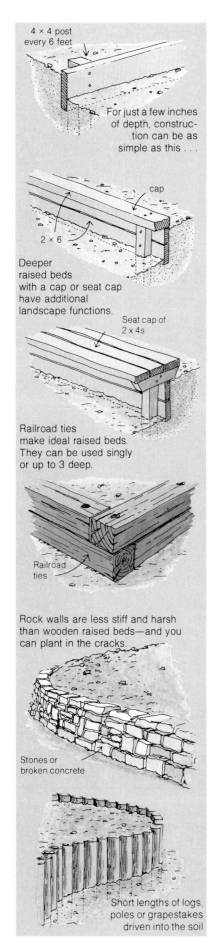

4 × 4 post every 6 feet

For just a few inches of depth, construction can be as simple as this . . .

cap

2 × 6

Deeper raised beds with a cap or seat cap have additional landscape functions.

Seat cap of 2 x 4s

Railroad ties make ideal raised beds. They can be used singly or up to 3 deep.

Railroad ties

Rock walls are less stiff and harsh than wooden raised beds—and you can plant in the cracks.

Stones or broken concrete

Short lengths of logs, poles or grapestakes driven into the soil

A container gardener is more likely to plant a succession of a few green onions and a few heads of lettuce than a dirt gardener will.

Planting for a succession of harvests with boxes is the very best way to approach planting a 3' x 9' garden or a 10' x 20' garden. (See "Planning the Garden," pages 42-47.)

If you are an inquisitive gardener, you'll find that container gardening gives you new freedom. Where the dirt gardener might hesitate to plant 1 trial sweet potato, 3 or 4 peanut seeds, ½ dozen shallots or multiplier onions, 2 or 3 miniature varieties of cabbage, or 1 small lemon cucumber, as a container gardener you can always find room for another pot or box.

A container gardener can change the climate more easily than a dirt gardener can. If your climate is too cool for eggplant, for example, you can move the container next to your house; the wall's reflected heat may give the eggplant all the extra heat it needs to produce fruits.

Growing vegetables in containers offers many advantages from the standpoint of early harvest, as well. When you use a commercial planter mix as your soil, you can plant when it's time to plant. You don't have to wait for rain-soaked soil to dry out. It's easy to protect a planter box from wind and frost. And a sterilized planter mix to keep plants free from damage by nematodes and soil-borne diseases.

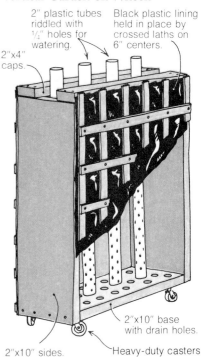

Vertical Garden on Wheels

2" plastic tubes riddled with ¼" holes for watering.

Black plastic lining held in place by crossed laths on 6" centers.

2"x4" caps.

2"x10" base with drain holes.

2"x10" sides.

Heavy-duty casters

Fill with soil mix. Cut holes through plastic to insert small plants.

Above: Experiments with a vertical roll-around box have proven successful in achieving gardening space where no land is available. Since it can be rolled around, both sides of the planter can be planted and turned to the sun, as needed. Left: Lettuce has the form and color required for pattern planting. Even patterns as complex as the traditional "knot gardens" can be achieved.

Opposite, top and center: Examples of small space gardens.

A strawberry container offers another kind of harvest when planted with Japanese cucumber, herbs, and pink banana squash.

When plants are crowded in containers, compensate for the lack of root space with frequent light liquid feedings.

Remember your neighbors. If you plant a balcony garden and there is a balcony below you, don't forget that water drips. Put saucers under pots and a floor of black plastic film under planters, and your relations with your downstairs neighbors will stay friendly.

When using solid plastic pails and trash containers, don't forget to provide for drainage. Drill evenly spaced holes along the sides and near the bottom. (But don't drill holes in the bottom itself. The soil would drain out along with the water.)

You can use bags of Jiffy Mix, Pro-Mix, Peat-Lite, and other lightweight mixes that are packaged in plastic bags as leak-proof planters on decks and balconies. Simply cut slits for planting "holes." Add water until all the mix is wet. Don't overwater to the point of sogginess. Set in your transplants of lettuce, tomatoes, or whatever. Plants grown in these mixes require watering far less often than those grown in pots or boxes. Even in the plastic bags, these lightweight mixes maintain good aeration.

If you think we are exaggerating the possibilities and enjoyments of growing vegetables without a garden, send for the U.S.D.A. Bulletin No. 163, *Mini-Gardens for Vegetables* .

EXPERIENCED ADVICE

From one season to the next a gardener picks up, and occasionally invents, new solutions to common garden problems. On these pages we explore solutions as well as some old-fashioned good ideas.

Seemingly minor tips can make a sizable difference in the amount of pleasure you receive from gardening. And there's nothing that makes the novice gardener feel more like a pro than passing the tip on to another gardener. The list of ideas and helpful hints received from gardeners was a long one: the following are some considered particularly useful.

"What variety is that?" "We try out new varieties in a rather cautious fashion. The trial plantings are small in comparison to the ones we have had success with. To make sure that we have the name of the variety at harvest time, we keep a record on a garden map or on stakes.

"Seed packets on stakes quickly fade out in rain or sprinkling or get lost. We've tried several methods—from writing on stakes with a waterproof marker to protecting the seed packet. You can put the seed packet or the written label between sheets of plastic (art supply stores carry plastic sheets suitable for this purpose). Or cover the package with a mat-surface, scotch-type tape. Or use lacquer in a spray can. Fasten the packet or label to the stake with double-sided tape or white glue."

Clothespins. "Spring-clip clothespins are useful when handling seed packets in the garden. Clip them on partly used packets—fold the top back—so the rest of the seeds won't spill out."

Parcel post storage. "We mounted the large parcel-post-size mailbox on a 5-foot-high post alongside the main path in the garden. It gives us handy storage for insecticides, gadgets, twine, small tools, markers, and the like. It's weatherproof and high enough to keep things out of reach of small children. This year we trained a cucumber to climb up the post."

Old rule. *A seed company told us:* "When seeds fail to germinate, some gardeners are sure that the fault must be in the seed. Actually it's almost impossible to buy seed that will not germinate. It is not uncommon to see 90 percent or more of the seeds produce excellent plants. Gardeners do, and should, sow more seeds than are usually needed for the final stand. This excess is good insurance against less-than-perfect soil conditions and other hazards. The old rule for sowing corn, beans, and peas still has some validity: One for the blackbird, one for the crow, one for the cutworm and one to grow."

Indoor lettuce. An apartment dweller tells us: "I found that 'Ruby' leaf lettuce makes a beautiful house plant. I plant it in an 8-inch centerpiece bowl, water and fertilize it well and keep it near a window, and harvest a salad about once every 3 weeks all winter."

Plastic netting. "For the first time, we used plastic bird netting to protect newly planted corn, peas, and beans. We completely foiled such nuisance birds as brown thrashers, and for the first time in many years replanting was unnecessary."

Black plastic stops weeds, acts as a mulch and slows evaporation. It increases yields of many warm weather crops, especially melons.

Coffee can waterer with holes punched in sides. No need to trench, no erosion, less weeds. Drains slowly, confines water to roots.

"Soaker" hose is very effective for watering young plants. It's portable and provides slow irrigation in long rows.

Raised beds for specialties. A gardener with all the space he wants to use has this to say: "I can't say enough for raised beds, and we will more than double the number we now use. They give me the ability to plant small quantities of certain vegetables without lousing up the garden rows. Specialties such as garlic (so little is needed) do well. We grow our shallots there, too, although we are about to double our planting and move them out into a full-size garden row. Raised beds are perfect for spring onions because you want only a few feet at a time. We have 2 of our beds reserved for herbs—1 for for perennials and the other for annuals."

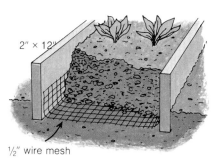

2" × 12"

1/2" wire mesh

Gopher protection. "Two families of gophers practically ruined our garden last year. This year we have gopher-proofed one section by building a 12-inch-deep raised bed and lining the bottom of the bed with ½-inch mesh wire."

Growing plants to set out. "I use an old styrofoam box—the kind you buy to keep things cool. Punch holes for drainage. Fill it half full with a mixture of 1 part soil, 1 part peat moss, and 1 part sand. Mix thoroughly. Place it on the south side of the house. Cover with a clear sheet of plastic. Remove the cover on warm days."

Coffee cans. "I am sure you have many ideas already. Hot caps I am not crazy about, as they can blow away if not carefuly anchored and they sometimes get the plant too hot. We have had good luck with respect to late, light frosts with 2-pound coffee cans that have both tops and bottoms removed. We put them over our tomatoes, eggplants, and peppers and leave them for a couple of weeks. Occasionally the tips of the leaves get burnt by the hot metal on contact but the damage is not permanent. We also use them on cabbage plants— not against frost but as protection against bugs. The advantage of the open-ended can is that you don't have to lift it off every morning and replace it again each night. Of course it's not protection against a heavy frost, but one would not normally be putting out tender plants that early, anyhow."

Bird protection. "I made a cover of aluminum fly screen. I built portable frames 14 inches wide, 7 inches high, and 9 feet long for my peas and beans, and smaller ones 7 inches wide for my carrots, beets, and lettuce. I store them in the winter and bring them out for the first seed sowing. They're very simple.

"The frames should be 1/2, 1/3 or 1/4 the length of a full row. Just staple the wire to the frame. A heavy stapling gun is ideal and very fast. The 7-inch-high frame is adequate. After the plants have reached 6 inches tall, birds don't do much damage. The first year we used 1-inch mesh chicken wire. It didn't stop the mice. Small birds squeezed through and couldn't get out again. But we've had no trouble after covering with the aluminum fly screen."

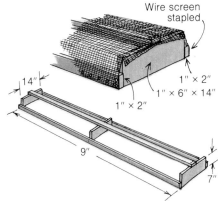

Wire screen stapled

14"

1" × 2"
1" × 6" × 14"
1" × 2"

9"

7"

Don't worry about clods. "Some gardeners work too hard spading and raking soil for a seed bed. I don't cheat on the depth of spading, but a few clods and small rocks don't bother me. When preparing seed bed for rows 2½ to 3 feet apart, I don't worry about clods between the rows.

"A clod-free strip can be developed quickly in very rough soil by hoeing up a ridge 4 to 6 inches high and then raking it down, pulling the clods off in the process. The row can be left slightly mounded if excess water is apt to be a problem."

Cone protection. "I have manufactured my own 'hot caps' by forming a cone out of plastic hardware cloth and a long pointed stick attached. It gives protection from frost and wind without danger of the heat build-up typical of hot caps. Furthermore, I can make the size fit the plant."

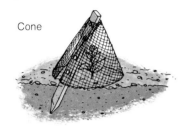
Cone

Little red wagon. "The little red wagon is a very practical gardening aid. In addition to using it to transport small tools, fertilizers, containers and such from the garage to the garden and back again, we also use it in early spring for indoor-outdoor movements of plants of pots in the transplant stage. We give them sunlight during the day and move them into the garage at night to protect them from frost."

Gallon-size plastic jugs with bottoms cut out are useful as mini-green-houses and insect protectors for tender young plants in cool areas.

Ice cream scoop. "For setting out transplants of lettuce, tomatoes, cabbage, and the like, I prefer the ice cream scoop over the trowel. I can get the same depth in each planting hole fast and easy."

Tomatoes and late frost. "We extend our tomato season by as much as 3 weeks by laying a wide strip of black plastic over each row at night. This year we will do the same with peppers and eggplants. Having frosts September 20th to 30th, we lose a lot of fruit unless we protect it this way."

More tomato training. "We solved the problem of keeping tomatoes off the ground without staking and very little tying and pruning. I built 2 frames to place over 12 plants, set 26 inches apart in a 27-foot row. They're rugged and have lasted 8 years. Here's a sketch of how they are made."

1" × 2" crosspiece
1" × 2" on edge mortised into leg
2" × 4" leg
One plant to each rectangle
Top view
End view

The start of a barrel of Chinese pod peas. In 2 or 3 months the plants will have grown up the strings to top point on stake.

Wood labels. "What works best for me are wooden marking stakes from the nursery. I mark them with an ordinary indelible pencil. They stay put in the ground better than plastic strips, and the writing doesn't smear. Over the winter I leave them face-up in the garden or another sunny spot—sun and moisture beach the indelible ink out of them by spring and I can reuse them."

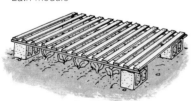
Lath module

Handy panels. "I hate to see transplants of anything wilt, even temporarily. So when transplanting the thinnings from lettuce, beets, and the like, I give them part shade for a few days. With small plants, I stick a shingle at an angle to stop the hot sun. The best protection is with latticed panels. I make them 2 feet wide and 3 feet long."

One way to keep a melon from getting sunburned. A simply constructed "A" frame, pictured, can be moved from place to place.

Watering many containers at once. "In hot windy weather, my son and I spent almost an hour watering our 24-plant container garden. The plants were in a light soil mix and we watered slowly. We tried putting a couple of inches of sand on top of the planter mix so we could water a little faster without floating the mix away. It helped, but our best idea was to use a length of galvanized eave trough (roof gutter) capped at both ends. "We laid it across the rims of a

Take the Worry Out of Watering

You can partially solve the problem of watering clay pots in the summer months or when vacation or business leaves the pots without a sitter. Many types of self-watering pots are available at your nursery or garden center, or you can work out your own, as illustrated below. A pot collection (where one pot protects the next one) is easier to care for than single-spaced pots. A simple temporary frame of boards around the grouping will protect the outside pots when you vacation-proof the garden.

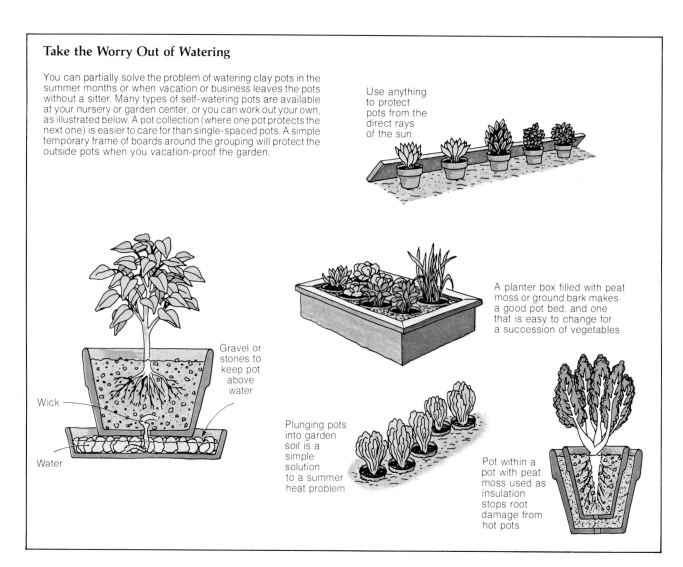

Use anything to protect pots from the direct rays of the sun

A planter box filled with peat moss or ground bark makes a good pot bed, and one that is easy to change for a succession of vegetables

Gravel or stones to keep pot above water

Wick

Water

Plunging pots into garden soil is a simple solution to a summer heat problem

Pot within a pot with peat moss used as insulation stops root damage from hot pots

dozen containers in a row and used a roofing nail to punch a hole in the bottom of the trough for each container. Now we flood the trough and it irrigates many pots at once. We also fertilize with liquid fertilizer this way. If we move a container out of the row, we plug up the unused water hole with liquid solder from a tube. During vacation, guardians find it easy to water properly."

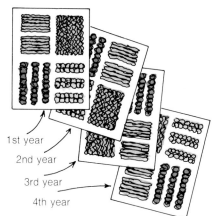

1st year
2nd year
3rd year
4th year

Rotation. "Recommended by everyone, like motherhood, but more difficult to achieve for the amateur. I have shown you my system of dividing the garden into quarters and planting all that was in quarter #1 this year in quarter #2 next year, etc. The acetate overlay I use with my garden layout is not so much for record keeping as it is for planning. I find it invaluable."

Hip-pocket tools. "For gardening in boxes and pots, the ordinary tools I could buy were too big and clumsy. I carry a 2-inch putty knife and a pair of scissors, and that's all. I can harvest beet greens, prune tomato plants, and thin carrots and lettuce by snipping rather than pulling. The putty knife is a spade, cultivator, and hoe all rolled into one. It's perfect for blocking out transplants in a flat."

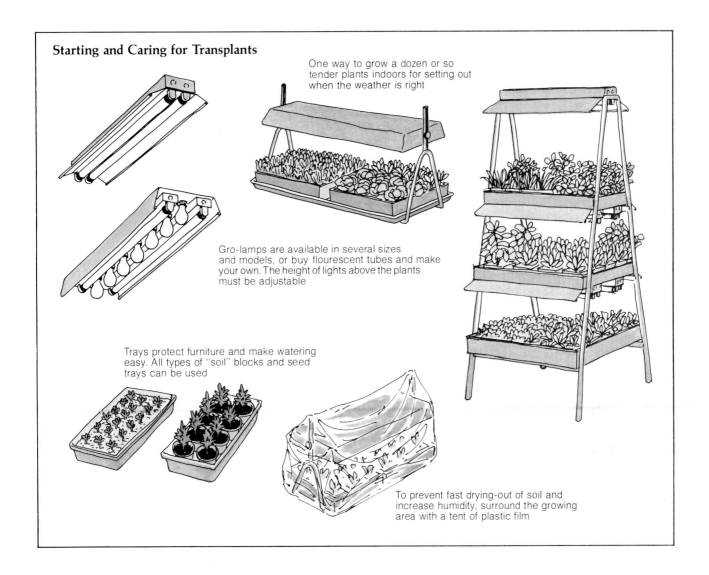

Starting and Caring for Transplants

One way to grow a dozen or so tender plants indoors for setting out when the weather is right

Gro-lamps are available in several sizes and models, or buy flourescent tubes and make your own. The height of lights above the plants must be adjustable

Trays protect furniture and make watering easy. All types of "soil" blocks and seed trays can be used

To prevent fast drying-out of soil and increase humidity, surround the growing area with a tent of plastic film

Nighttime warmth. "We built a plastic A-frame (see page 55) and found a way to keep it warm on cold nights. We put large plastic bleach bottles full of water inside the A-frame. The sun warms the water during the day. At night it slowly give off heat and keeps the A-frame several degrees warmer than the outside air."

Costs more—worth more. "The best investment I made in gardening equipment is the professional heavy-duty wheelbarrow. It's beautifully balanced and easy on the back. Moving dirt, compost, sand, peat moss—all bulky stuff— is no strain. And to the kids it's Pufer Bill's train and the magic garden ride."

No dirt, no worms. "I have found a way to bring smiles to the cook in the kitchen. The vegetables I bring in are really clean. After kitchen inspection there are no dirt or worms in the sink.

"I have a large pail of water and a wire basket, and I use either or both to suit the vegetable. Spray from the hose will take care of most of the dirt from root vegetables in the wire basket. Some may need to be washed in a pail. A couple of shakes and whirls in the wire basket gets rid of excess water."

An inside view of an artichoke reveals
symmetrical perfection, but gives little idea
of its delicious flavor.

ENCYCLOPEDIA OF VEGETABLES

On the following pages a close look is taken at both the common and uncommon vegetables—from artichokes to zucchini—that can be grown in most home gardens. If you can't find what you're looking for in alphabetical order, check the index.

In reading through the descriptions of the following vegetables, you'll probably end up wanting to plant more varieties than you have room for. While it is difficult to say what should and shouldn't be given space in a particular vegetable garden, from the point of view of maximum yield of food it doesn't make good sense to plant pumpkins, peanuts, and chayote if they crowd out lettuce, beets, carrots, and snap beans. However, when you consider the fun of growing something you have never grown before, it seems worthwhile to look for odd spaces to at least sample any vegetable that might appeal to you.

Artichoke

Centuries before Christ, the Romans paid top prices for this thistlelike vegetable and preserved it for year-round use. It disappeared with the fall of the Roman Empire and did not surface again until a thousand years later, in southern Italy. Catherine de Medici found artichokes in Florentine gardens and introduced them to France as gourmet delicacies. Artichokes came to America via French and Spanish explorers.

This perennial grows primarily in the cool, moist, coastal area between San Francisco and Santa Barbara. The harvest starts in late September and lasts until May. The buds are cut continually through the harvest period.

In its ornamental capacity, this handsome plant decorates gardens throughout the mild-winter areas of California and beyond.

You can buy dormant roots at nurseries in late winter or early spring, wherever this vegetable is adapted.

If you can't buy young plants, you can start with seed. Sow seed indoors, in peat pots, 4 to 6 weeks before it's time to set them out in the garden—after frost danger is passed.

The production of edible buds will depend upon spring and early summer weather. If summer heat comes early, the buds will open rapidly and become tough and leathery.

Where winters are cold in the fall, cut back the tops to 12 inches, tie the old stalks over the root crown, and cover with mulch. The common variety is 'Green Globe'. Catalog sources are (25), (26), (31).

Serving ideas. This beautiful thistle is beloved by Mediterranean peoples. Serve the tiny cooked hearts in a lemon, oil, and herb sauce. Stuff the large chokes with ground lamb, or serve them hot, Roman style—with long stems pointing upward and the flower ends down. Enhance them with hollandaise sauce, or marinate cold, cooked artichokes in a vinaigrette dressing.

Asparagus

The Romans grew asparagus as early as 200 B.C. They enjoyed this vegetable in season and dried it for later use.

The ancients knew its characteristics so well that the 1st-century Emperor

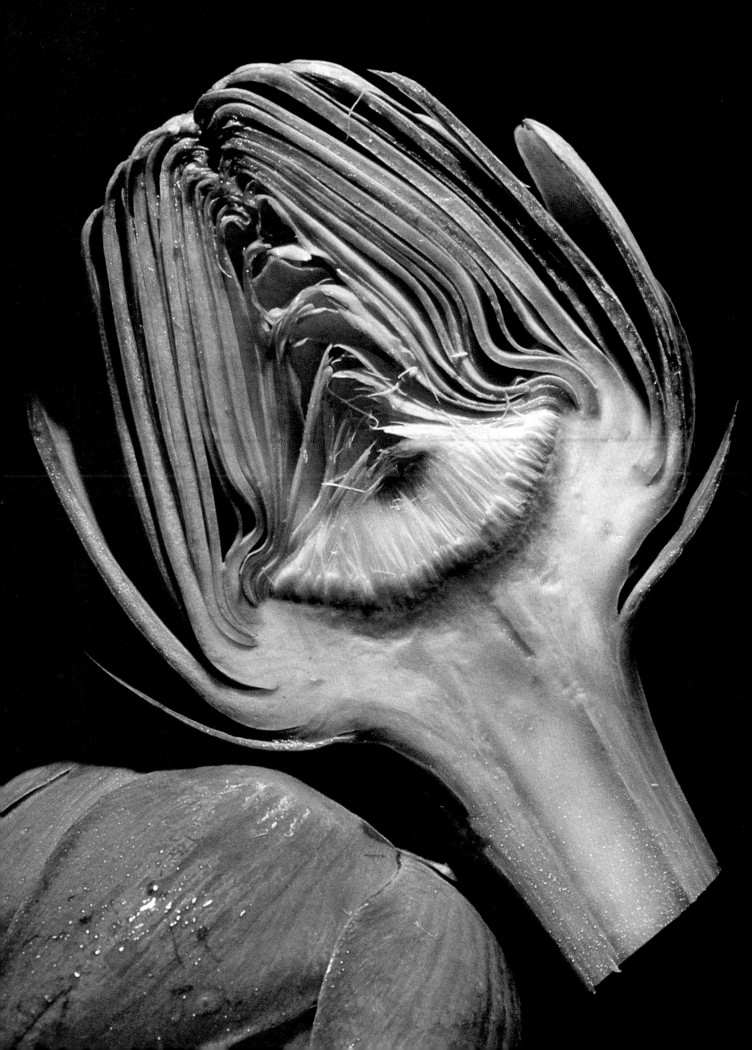

Asparagus spears are ready for harvesting when they are 6"-8" tall. Specially manufactured knives make the harvest easier.

Augustus defined the word "haste" as "quicker than you can cook asparagus."

Of "sperege," a 16th-century Englander said: "It is delicious eaten with oyl and vinegar." Records of plantings in American gardens attest to the long life of this vegetable. The 1917 Middlebury, Vermont *Register* tells us: "There is an asparagus bed on the Elios Lyman farm . . . which was started 101 years ago and continues to this day to yield a generous crop."

Growing asparagus demonstrates the fantastic growth power of Mother Nature. The asparagus is quite a manufacturing plant.

In summer, its graceful fernlike foliage stands tall and grows sunward. The leaves manufacture food beyond their growth needs and store this excess in the roots. The big transfer to storage comes when the tops die.

When the soil warms in the following spring, stalks rise from the crown to renew the plant. At this point, all growth occurs because of the food that's stored in the roots. (The manufacturing plant is on battery power.)

Since many more shoots form than the plant needs to renew itself, prune them—a few or more the first year, more the second. The third year should give you 4 weeks of cutting.

Prepare the soil. When you plant asparagus, you are building the foundation for 10 to 15 years of production. So take the time to work the soil a foot or more deep and to mix in large amounts of manure, compost, peat moss, or like organic material, plus 4 to 5 pounds of 5-10-10 fertilizer per 100 square feet.

Planting transplants (root crown). You save a year over starting from seed by buying 1-year-old plants (crowns) from garden centers or seed companies.

Dig trenches 8 inches deep and 4 to 5 feet apart. (Asparagus roots spread wide). Spread some compost or manure in the bottom of the trench and cover with an inch of garden soil.

Set the crowns 18 inches apart in the row, and cover with 2 inches of soil. As the new shoots come up, gradually fill in the trench.

Fertilizing. For high production and thick spears, follow a twice-a-year feeding program. To encourage heavy top growth, make the first application before growth starts in the spring, and the second as soon as the harvest is finished. Don't skimp on water when the top growth is developing.

Harvesting. Cut or snap off spears when they are 6 to 8 inches high. "Snapping"—bending the spear over sharply until it breaks—avoids injuring other shoots below ground. Or use an asparagus knife to cut the spears.

Early in the season, the shoots may require cutting only every third day; but as the growth becomes more active you may have to cut twice a day, especially if the asparagus is growing in very light, warm soil.

Varieties. Choose rust-resistant varieties such as 'Mary Washington' and 'Waltham Washington'.

Serving ideas. Fresh young asparagus is excellent raw, added to green salads in thin, diagonal slices, or included on a relish platter with a sour cream dip. Or nestle asparagus spears in a basket of *crudités*: fresh raw vegetables arranged like a nosegay in a small wicker basket. Serve with mayonnaise or a French *tapenade* sauce: mayonnaise seasoned with chopped ripe olives and anchovies.

Set crowns in trench 18" apart—spread roots so they lie flat...

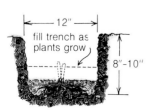

Asparagus in summer

12"
fill trench as plants grow
8"-10"

Serve hot cooked asparagus spears Dutch-style, with browned butter, sieved egg yolk, and chopped watercress.

Beans

Although beans originated in Central America, they already existed in many parts of the western hemisphere by the time Columbus arrived. Several varieties we use today were developed by the American Indians.

The planting chart on page 56 gives directions on planting these beans: snaps, bush and pole; limas, bush and pole; fava beans; garbanzos; scarlet runners; soybeans; and yardlong beans. All are discussed here except soybeans (page 123) and yardlongs (page 139).

Snap beans are said to be the foolproof vegetable for the beginning gardener: they are easy to grow—but not foolproof.

Time to sow seeds in place (can be started indoors 3 weeks earlier)

Zone/South	Zone/North	Zone/West
1 1/1-4/1, 9/1-12/31	**5** 4/10-5/30, 7/1-8/15	**6, 8, 13** 5/15-7/15
2 2/1-4/1, 8/14-9/30	**6** 4/15-6/15, 7/10-8/10	**9** 5/15-6/30
3 3/1-4/30, 8/1-9/15	**7** 5/1-6/30	**10** 5/20-6/15
4 3/15-5/31, 7/1-8/15	**8** 5/10-8/10	**12** 5/10-6/30
5 4/1-5/31, 7/1-8/10	**9** 5/15-6/30	**14** 1/1-3/31, 8/1-31
6 4/15-5/31, 7/1-31	**10** 5/20-6/15	**15, 21** 2/1-5/31
7 5/15-6/30	**11** 5/20-6/1	**16** 5/10-7/10
13 5/15-7/15		**18** 5/1-7/30
		19 1/1-8/30
		20 4/15-6/30
		22 4/1-5/30, 7/1-7/31

Yellow wax bean

Purple-podded pole bean

Mistakes Beginners Make. *Planting too early.* Seeds will not germinate in cold soil. If you want to rush the season, sow the seeds indoors in peat pots and set them out when the soil warms up.

Planting too deep or too shallow. In spring, plant no more than 1 inch deep. In summer plantings, increase the depth in follow-up plantings to 2 inches.

Allowing soil to crust over. A sprouting bean must pull folded leaves through the soil and spread them aboveground. When the soil is crusted or heavy, the sprout can't get through—broken shoots show where the sprout has tried and failed.

To prevent crusting, apply a light mulch over the seed row; or, if a crust forms at emergence time, soften it with a light sprinkling. If your soil is heavy clay, make deep furrows and fill them with planter soil mix, not only to prevent crusting but also to give the beans an extra-early lift.

Leaving overmature pods on the vines. To get a full crop of snap beans, pick the beans before the large seeds develop. Leaving a few old pods on a plant will

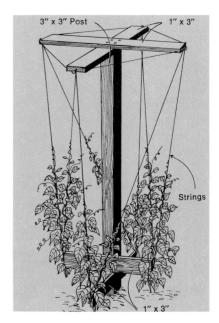

Above and below: Scarlet runner beans are rampant growers. You'll frequently find them listed as a flowering vine instead of a vegetable, but if picked when young, they can be eaten as string beans.

greatly reduce the set of new ones. Snap beans should be picked in the young, succulent stage.

Letting soil dry out. Lack of moisture in the soil will cause the plant to produce "pollywogs"—only the first few seeds develop and the rest of the pod shrivels to a tail.

Failing to feed bush beans early enough in the season. The plant must make strong early growth so that it's of good size before flowering starts. So feed before planting: mix a 5-10-10 fertilizer at the rate of 3 pounds per 100 square feet into the soil.

With pole beans, you must feed and water continually. It's possible to get a second crop after the main crop is finished. Remove all pods, fertilize, and water deeply.

Types Of Beans

Bush beans. These beans need only about 60 days of moderate temperatures to produce a crop of green pods. Because of their short growth-period, they can be grown nearly anywhere in the United States. If you make small plantings every 2 weeks, you can keep them coming to the kitchen over many months in most areas.

There are many varieties of green bush beans. Near the top of all recommended lists are: 'Tendercrop' (53 days to maturity); 'Topcrop' (49 days); 'Bush Blue Lake' (58 days); 'Tendergreen' (56 days); 'Spartan Arrow' (52 days); 'Greensleeves' (56 days); 'Tenderette' (53 days); 'Provider' (50 days); 'Contender' (48 days); 'Commodore' (58 days); 'Harvester' (60 days), and 'Tenderpod' (58 days).

'Romano 14' (52 days) is a bush form of the popular pole variety, 'Romano'. The large broad flat pods are as thick, succulent and flavorful as the regular Romano.

The bush wax beans most frequently recommended are: 'Resistant Kinghorn Wax' (54 days); 'Cherokee Wax' (52 days); 'Pencil Pod Wax' (54 days); 'Burpee's Brittle Wax' (52 days); 'Goldcrop' (54 days); and 'Golden Wax Improved' (50 days).

Purple-podded 'Royalty' (55 days). This tender, stringless, purple-podded bush bean is gaining a reputation for flavor and ability to grow in colder soil than other snap beans. Furthermore, bean beetles seem to avoid it. When cooked in boiling water for 2 minutes, the pods turn deep green, providing a built-in indicator of doneness for home freezing.

Pole snap beans. If you are a small-space gardener, you may find that going vertical with a trellis, teepee, or fence of pole beans solves your garden planning better than a succession of bush beans. And pole beans will give you production over a longer period.

'Kentucky Wonder' is still the favorite. 'Blue Lake' is praised for its thick flesh and small, slow-maturing seeds. The variety 'Ramona,' a broad flat bean of distinctive flavor, is increasing in popularity.

Lima beans. These beans require warmer soils to germinate properly, and higher temperatures and a longer season to produce a crop. But if the weather is extremely hot, these beans will fail to set pods.

Of the bush lima varieties, 'Fordhook 242' (70 days) is widely adapted and sets pods under higher temperatures than most varieties. 'Henderson Bush' (65 days) is a good producer of small baby limas.

The popular pole lima variety is still the old-timer, 'King of the Garden'.

Horticulture beans. These large-seeded beans are grown to be used when the beans themselves are in the green-shell stage; the fiber of the pod is too tough to be cooked as snap beans. The pods are colorful, striped, and mottled in red. You can find displays of them at county fairs. The 'Dwarf Horticultural' bean (65 days to green-shell stage) is light green in the snap stage, and marked with carmine at maturity.

Varieties are 'Dwarf Horticultural' and 'Bush Horticultural'. The pole variety is 'King Horticultural'. Seed sources are: (13), (26), (28), and (44).

Broadbeans, favas, horsebeans, and Windsors. These are not true beans but are related to vetch. They will grow in cool weather unsuitable for snapbeans. In mild-winter areas, they are planted in the fall for a spring crop. They will not produce in summer heat.

The varieties 'Long Pod' and 'Broad Long Pod' have 5 to 7 large, flat seeds and can be used as a substitute for pole limas, green-shell or dry, in short-season areas.

Garbanzo beans. Botanically, garbanzos are neither beans nor peas but *Cicer arietinum*, chick pea or gram. The gram is as much a food staple in India as the bean is in the United States.

Garbanzo, a bush type, produces 1 or 2 seeds in each puffy little pod. Pick it in the green-ripe stage, or let it ripen for dry beans. When cooked, garbanzos have a chestnutlike flavor and add a pleasant touch to a green salad or a mixed bean salad. The puréed cooked beans are notable blended with garlic, lemon juice, and sesame paste in an Arabian dip.

Serving ideas. Many cuisines throughout the world depend on fresh and dried beans as a staple food. These legumes vary greatly in size and style of cooking. Many are available in both fresh and dried form.

When cooking with dried beans, you don't have to soak them overnight. For a shortcut, place them in a kettle, cover with water, and bring to a quick boil. Boil for 2 minutes, remove from heat, and allow to stand 1 hour, still covered with water. Then cook until tender, according to your recipe.

You can cook runner, lima, and pinto beans in a similar fashion—in boiling salted water, just until tender.

For broadbeans, peel the shelled beans, then cook in boiling salted water. Serve hot with butter or puréed with heavy cream.

Beets

The beet originally came from the Mediterranean, where it grew as a leafy form, without enlarged roots. Today, improved types of these early beets are grown as Swiss chard. Large-rooted beets first were noted in literature around 1550 in Germany, but in 1806 in the U.S., only one variety was listed.

How to grow. Plant beets directly, in rows a foot or more apart. Thin them to 2 inches. You can postpone some of the thinning until the extra plants are large enough to eat—greens, roots, and all. Unless you use a monogerm

Romano pole beans

A golden beet, and the more traditional dark red variety.

(single-seeded) variety, each beet seedball will produce 3 to 5 plants in a tight clump, so thin them early.

Though beets prefer cool weather, they are tolerant of a wide range of conditions. The planting date chart shows that they can be planted early, but you can make additional plantings for a long time. In very hot weather, give special attention to watering and mulching to give the seedlings a good stand.

Mistakes beginners make. As usual, overplanting and underthinning are the most common mistakes. If there is not enough moisture, or if weeds or other beets compete, your beets will be stringy and tough. Beets must be grown full-speed without a single let-up.

Time to sow seeds in place

Zone/South		Zone/North		Zone/West	
1	1/1-2/28. 10/1-12/31	5	3/15-5/15	**6, 8, 13,** 3/20-6/30	
2	1/1-3/15. 9/1-11/10	6	3/20-5/30	9	4/15-6/10
3	1/15-3/31. 8/15-9/31	7	4/1-6/10	10	5/1-6/10
4	2/15-4/30. 8/1-9/15	8	4/15-6/15	12	4/1-5/10
5	3/1-4/30. 8/1-9/1	9	4/15-6/10	14	1/1-1/30. 9/1-12/31
6	2/15-5/15. 7/15-8/20	10	5/1-6/10	**15, 21** 2/1-8/30	
7	4/1-6/15	11	5/1-5/20	**16, 17** 3/20-7/20	
13	3/20-6/30			18	2/1-8/30
				19	2/1-8/30
				20	2/1-8/30
				22	2/1-8/30

Varieties. Which varieties you decide on for garden use is not very critical. But you do need to choose plants with downy-mildew resistance. All varieties can serve both for roots and greens, but if you need greens to any extent, plant chard or a variety of beets designed for that use. If you can find the seed, sugar beets are excellent for greens.

'Detroit Dark Red' (63 days). Dark color, neat globe shape. Downy-mildew-resistant strains are available.

'Early Wonder' (55 days). Semiglobe.

'Ruby Queen' (60 days). Globe, deep red.

'Mono-King Explorer' (50 days). This deep red, monogerm type has a single seed to each seedball.

'Burpee Golden' (55 days). This good-quality root has an unusual golden-yellow color. It may average higher in sugar. The pigment does not bleed out in cooking, as occurs with red beets.

Beets for greens listed by various catalogs include: Sugar Beets, 'Green Top Bunching', Beets For Greens, 'White Beet', and 'Lutz Green Leaf'.

Serving ideas. Serve hot, cooked, sliced beets in an orange sauce or with dollops of sour cream. Shred raw beets and cook quickly in butter. Cooked beets are good in herring salad or borsch.

A tight compact head of broccoli, ready for picking.

Broccoli

Sprouting broccoli, grown like cabbage, is more tolerant of heat than cauliflower. Broccoli can be harvested over a long period. After you've cut the center cluster of buds, side shoots will develop clusters for some time.

Time to sow seeds in place (for dates, see Cabbage, page 82).

Varieties. Strains of 'Italian Green Sprouting'—'De Cicco' (65 days) and 'Calabrese' (65 days)—are widely available. Frequently recommended varieties are: 'Green Comet' (55 days); 'Spartan Early' (55 days); 'Waltham 29' (74 days); 'Premium Crop', All-America Selection, (58 days); 'Green Duke' (68 days); 'Cleopatra', All-America Selection, (53 days).

Brussels Sprouts

Sprouts require cool weather and are best grown for fall and winter harvest. Set out transplants in June or July.

The sprouts mature in sequence as long as weather permits. Remove the leaves from beneath the lowest sprouts and twist them off. The sprouts above will continue to develop.

In cold-winter areas you can make sure of a full harvest by pinching out the growing tip in early fall. All the sprouts will be ready about the same time.

The principal varieties are 'Jade Cross Hybrid' (95 days) and 'Long Island Improved' (90 days).

Time to sow seeds in place (for dates, see Cabbage, page 82)

Serving ideas. Boil these diminutive mild cabbages and dress them with butter or sour cream, or turn them into a nutmeg-sprinkled cream sauce or cheese sauce. For an interesting Oriental stir-fry, combine sprouts and thinly sliced beef, and season with soy sauce and fresh ginger root.

Cabbage

Cabbage as we know it developed gradually from leafy, nonheading forms that grew wild in various parts of Europe. Hard-heading types were not definitely recorded until 1536. They were introduced to the New World in 1541.

How to grow. Plan for a succession of a few heads at a time. Buy transplants for the earliest planting, then sow the seeds directly in the garden for follow-up crops.

To produce large heads, space plants 20 inches or more in rows 36 inches apart. For smaller, normally developed heads big enough for family use, space the plants 12 inches apart.

Cabbage is a heavy user of nitrogen and potash. Before planting, add 6 to 8 pounds of 5-10-10 for 100 square feet and work it into the soil. In 3 to 4 weeks, follow up with a side dressing of about 1 pound of ammonium nitrate per 100 feet of row.

Problems. Since the heads of early varieties split soon after they mature in warm weather, at any one time plant only the number you can use in a 2- to 3-week period.

To slow up splitting, hold off on water, partially root prune the plant when the heads are formed, or simply twist the plant to break some of the roots. Splitting is seldom a problem with late varieties maturing in cool weather.

A number of our gardeners reported trouble: young plants bolted and over-wintering plants failed to form heads.

Leave plenty of room between the plants if you want large heads of cabbage.

Plant for color and texture in your garden. Here are 'Ruby Ball' cabbage and bright marigolds. This planting grew through the days of July and August without bolting or splitting. "Ruby" is the color of the cabbage head.

There are many types of cabbage: varieties with flat heads, round heads, pointed heads, green, white, and red heads. They vary in weight from 2½ to 8 pounds, and mature in anywhere from 65 to 105 days.

Cabbage is a biennial, forming a leafy head the first year and flowering the second. The change from leaf stage to flowering (bolting) will occur in young plants if they are exposed to temperatures below 50° for 2 or 3 weeks. Large transplants, subjected to low winter temperatures, will flower in the spring. You will have less trouble with bolting if you use transplants whose stems are the size of a lead pencil.

Time to sow seeds in place (sow seeds indoors 5-7 weeks earlier)

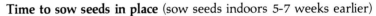

Zone/South	Zone/North	Zone/West
1 1/1-3/1, 9/1-12/31	**5** 3/1-4/15, 6/10-8/10	**6, 8, 13** 4/1-6/3
2 1/1-2/28, 8/15-9/30	**6** 3/5-4/5, 6/1-7/31	**9** 5/1-6/15
3 1/15-3/15, 8/1-9/30	**7** 3/15-4/15, 5/15-7/15	**10** 5/5-6/15
4 2/1-3/30, 7/15-8/30	**8** 4/1-5/15	**12** 4/1-5/31
5 2/10-4/5, 6/1-8/15	**9** 5/1-6/15	**14** 9/1-11/30
6 3/1-4/15, 6/1-7/31	**10** 5/5-6/15	**15, 21** 1/1-2/28, 10/1-12/31
7 3/15-4/15, 6/1-7/31	**11** 5/1-5/20	**16, 17** 4/1-7/10
13 4/1-6/3		**18** 1/1-4/30, 7/1-9/30
		19 1/1-2/28, 9/1-11/30
		20 1/1-4/30, 7/1-9/30
		22 1/1-2/28, 7/1-7/31

Varieties. Varieties that are yellows resistant are indicated (YR).

Early to medium. 'Early Jersey Wakefield' (63) days. (YR). 2½ to 3 pounds.

'Golden Acre' (64 days). (YR). 4 to 5 pounds. Quick to split.

'Copenhagen Market' (72 days). (YR). 4 to 4½ pounds.

'Marion Market' (75 days). (YR). 5½ to 7 pounds.

'Stonehead' (70 days). 5 pounds. All-America selection.

'Market Prize' (76 days). (YR). 4 to 5 pounds.

'Harvester Queen' (60 days). (YR). 5 pounds. All-America Selection.

'Savoy Ace' (85 days). 4 to 4½ pounds. All-America Selection.

'Red Head' (80 days). 4 pounds. All-America Selection.

'Emerald Cross' (63 days). 4 to 6 pounds. All-America Selection.

'Ruby Ball' (68 days). 4 to 6 pounds. All-America Selection.

Late. 'Danish Ballhead' (105 days).

Red. 'Red Acre' (76 days). 4 pounds. Slow to split.

'Red Danish Ballhead' (97 days). 5 pounds.

Savoy. 'Chieftain Savoy' (88 days). Standard savoy, densely curled, crumpled leaves.

'Savoy King' (90 days). (YR). 4 pounds. All-America Selection.

The midgets. 'Dwarf Morden' (53 days). (YR). Firm, round, tender 4-inch heads. Seed sources: (9), (21), and (26). See page 140.

'Little Leaguer Cabbage' (60 days). Round, 4-inch, softball-sized heads.

'Baby Head' (72 days). Very small. 2½- to 3- pound heads. Holds well without splitting. Hard as a rock. Thick leaves. Seed source: (27).

Cabbage color. If you want color in the late fall and early winter, sow seed or set out transplants of ornamental kale or cabbage. We planted a small plot of ornamental cabbage in August, and the mixtures of colors and shapes out-rivaled everything else in the garden. Give ornamental cabbage the same culture as you would edible cabbages. Both the dwarf size and the regular size are available. Nichols Nursery (19) describes the "Miniature Japanese Ornamental Cabbage" this way: "Tiny plants look like giant roses, in lovely deep red shades on green. Make nice pot plants. Used for making color patches in garden. Plants need cold weather to bring out their variegated colors. Gives salads nice color combination."

Serving ideas. A combination of both white and red cabbage, shredded, makes a striking coleslaw. Add fresh pineapple chunks or diced apple, if you wish.

Include this leafy vegetable in a classic French *pot-au-feu* and Spanish and Italian boiled dinners. Stuff the head with ground pork and veal in the Danish manner, or turn it into a Hungarian strudel. Offer it sweet and sour, German-style, or follow the Normandy method, shredding and cooking it with apple slices to accompany duck.

Pickle it for sauerkraut to savor in such diverse dishes as the French *choucroute garni* (sauerkraut with pork and sausages), Russian sauerkraut soup, and Hungarian layered pork and sauerkraut.

Cardoon

This native of the Mediterranean is closely related to the globe artichoke, which it resembles in general appearance. Both are like big ornamental 3- to 4-foot thistles with deeply cut leaves, a crown that multiplies by sending out side branches, and a heavy flower head flaunting purple bristles on the thistles. But while the globe artichoke is raised primarily for its fleshy flower bud, cardoon is grown for the young leafstalks, which are blanched and eaten like celery in salads and soups.

In the garden, plant seeds in late April; indoors, plant in pots in March for setting out in May. The large plants need space—18 inches between plants, with 3 to 4 feet between rows. Cardoon sometimes is planted in the bottom of a 1-foot-deep trench. In September, when the plants are large, tie the leaves together in a bunch, wrap them with paper or burlap, and mound them up with soil to blanch the leafstalks. It takes about a month for adequate blanching.

Cardoon needs plentiful feeding and watering to grow vigorously, otherwise the leafstalks may get pithy and the plant may flower.

Cut off the blanched plants just below the crown, and trim off the outside leaves. A blanched heart, some 18 to 24 inches in length, will remain. Cut the stalks of this heart into sections, then parboil them for 1½ hours until they become tender and lose their bitterness.

Some catalogs offer the spineless varieties 'Large Smooth', 'Ivory White Smooth', and 'Large Smooth Spanish'. Check catalogs: (7), (19), (25).

Serving ideas. The Italians, who are partial to this vegetable, blanch the stalks and then serve them chilled, dressed with oil and wine vinegar, or hot, topped with a cream sauce and croutons. Sometimes chunks of cardoon are batter-dipped and deep-fried until crispy.

A close relative of the artichoke, cardoon is grown for its young leaf stalks.

Carrots

Carrots originated from wild forms grown around the Mediterranean. They were well established as a food in Europe by the 13th century. In the 17th century they came to America with the first settlers, and Indians soon began growing them.

Carrots adapt well, tolerate mismanagement, and supply food for an admirably long time, using nothing more for storage than the soil in which they are grown.

How to grow. The Nichols Nursery Catalog offers this advice: "How to raise carrots without using a spade or hoe. It is simple, and here is how it is done: Build a raised bed made of 2 x 8 lumber (length optional) but width should not exceed 4 feet. Fill bed with 1/5 garden loam, 2/5ths clean sand and 2/5 compost, rotted manure, or peat moss. For every 10 feet length of bed spread 5 pounds of bone meal. Mix all ingredients thoroughly, then rake down into a fine seed bed. Broadcast the carrot seed, cover with 1/4 inch fine sifted peat moss. Water, and keep bed well moistened, but not soggy wet. Pull carrots as they are ready. July sown seed will give you carrots in the fall."

We agree. We only question the inclusion of manure in the soil mix. Unless they are very well rotted, manures make carrots rough and branching.

Raised beds reduce cracking and decay problems caused by excess water in the fall. The light soil mix makes it easy to dig. The soil warms up early in raised beds, and you can start carrots earlier than in the regular garden soil.

See chapters on sowing seed (page 48) and planning the garden (page 42) for specifics on handling carrots.

Time to sow seeds in place (for dates, see Beets, page 80).

Varieties. Choose varieties according to your preference for shape and size. The short-to-medium or very short types do better in heavy or rough soils than the long types do, and are easier to dig, as well.

Short-to-medium. Good for wet fall and winter and heavy soils.

'Red Cored Chantenay' (70 days to maturity). Medium length, heavy, widely adapted.

'Royal Chantenay' (70 days). Longer than Red Cored Chantenay. An improved strain.

'Spartan Bonus' (75 days). Medium long and heavy; good producer.

'Danvers Half Long' (75 days). Bright orange, heavy producer.

Long, slender. Better in light sandy soils, need deep loose soils.

'Nantes'. Good quality, cracks in wet fall weather.

'Imperator' (75 days). Standard market carrot, 8 to 9 inches long, good quality.

'Gold Pak' (76 days). Deep color, 8 to 9 inches long.

Very short. 'Oxheart' (75 days). Good for heavy soils. Plump and short.

Serving ideas. This popular, brilliant vegetable is found in many cuisines in a range of dishes, from appetizers to desserts. Include diagonally sliced carrots on the *Bagna Cauda* tray. Carrots lend color to many international stews and boiled dinners. They are a surprise ingredient in continental nut cakes.

Cauliflower

More demanding than broccoli or cabbage, cauliflower will not head up properly in hot weather and cannot stand as much cold as cabbage. Its culture and planting dates are generally the same as for cabbage.

When the curds (heads) develop and begin to show through the leaves, it's time to blanch them. Gather the leaves together over the curd and tie them off with soft twine or plastic strips.

Time to sow seeds in place (for dates, see Cabbage, page 82).

Varieties. Strains of 'Snowball' are the most practical: 'Early Snowball' (60 days). 'Snowball Y' (68 days). 'Snow King' (50 days); All-America Selection.

A bountiful harvest of straight carrots is a sure sign of deep, fine-textured soil. Below: There are many varieties of carrots. If your soil has a dense structure, favor the shorter varieties.

'Snow Crown' (53 days); All-America Selection. 'Super Snowball' (58 days).

'Purple Head' (85 days). Large heads. Turns green when cooked. No need to blanch.

Cauliflower, a member of the cabbage family, deserves wider popularity. It is particularly flavorful when marinated raw.

Serving ideas. Raw cauliflowerets are ideal for dips and the Italian *Bagna Cauda*, an anchovy-garlic-butter sauce.

Steam the cauliflowerets and serve hot with a delicate nutmeg-spiced cheese sauce in the Scandinavian manner.

Cook cauliflower Greek-style—whole and coated with a mixture of 3 parts olive oil to 1 part lemon juice. Sprinkle lightly with oregano. Place on a platter and surround with hot baby artichoke hearts.

Celeriac

This form of celery is grown for its swollen root. The plant is smaller than celery, and the foliage is a very dark green.

Grow in the same way as celery. Celeriac needs just as much high fertilizing and as continuous a supply of water.

Serving ideas. Mix raw julienne strips of celery root with apple, tongue, and chicken for a Dutch-style luncheon salad. Dress with vinaigrette and garnish

Celeriac

Not for every garden, celery makes special demands on the gardener. But for some, the extra effort is worth it.

Unlike lettuce, you want celtuce plants to go to seed.

with tomato wedges and egg slices. Or shred the raw root, toss it in an oil and vinegar dressing, and garnish with watercress and olives.

Mingle cooked sliced celery root with cooked shrimp in a mustard-scented vinaigrette on a bed of butter lettuce and watercress.

For a Bavarian soup, include celery root in a beef shank soup with leeks. Or add the root to the famous Greek Easter lemon soup, *Mageritsa*.

Celery

This member of the parsley family probably originated near the Mediterranean, but wild forms of it grow in wet places all over Europe and across southern Asia. In ancient times it was used as a medicine, and not until around 1600 did it start to be used as food. During this time, celery had hollow, fibrous, strong-flavored stalks that had to be blanched to be made edible. Modern celery, on the other hand, is solid, relatively free from fiber, mild, and edible in its natural green state.

How to grow. Celery demands more time and attention than most vegetables. If you start from seed you should have a 10- to 12-week growing period indoors and a 120-day period in the garden. Otherwise you can buy seedlings from a garden center and transplant directly to the garden.

Sow the very small seeds ⅛-inch deep. Keep them moist by covering the flats or pots with moist burlap until emergence starts. Transplant carefully: supply shade and water to reduce stress on the plants.

Apply fertilizer heavily—as much as 16 pounds of 5-10-10 per 100 feet of row. Mix these quantities thoroughly into a wide row (18 to 24 inches) to avoid burning.

Celery needs an abundant and continuous water supply.

The modern varieties don't usually require blanching, but if you want to do this, wrap the celery with paper or shade it with boards.

Varieties. Celery is a biennial plant that can be induced to flower rather easily —simply expose the young plants to cold weather.

Choose one of the following slow-bolting varieties for early spring planting:

'Summer Pascal' (115 days to maturity). Medium-green type, very thick stalks.

'Golden Self Blanching' (115 days). Lighter color, less thick than 'Summer Pascal'.

For late spring or summer planting where bolting would not be a problem, choose one of these varieties:

'Utah 52-70' (125 days). Dark green, thick stalks. The leading variety of this type in the U.S.

'Giant Pascal' (125 days). Good storage, large heart, thick stalks.

(Mature celery left to overwinter will produce great quantities of seed that can be harvested and used for flavoring purposes.)

Serving ideas. Serve it raw as a relish, spread with blue or cream cheese spreads. Or use it on a raw vegetable platter to dip into such spreads as clam dip, guacamole, and onion and sour cream dip. Or include it on a *Bagna Cauda* tray. It adds crunch to numerous salads, especially shrimp, crab, chicken, and Waldorf.

Serve it hot, with anchovy fillets and wine vinegar. Or braise and chill it, then dress with vinaigrette for Celery Victor. Include diagonal slices in fast stir-fries with shrimp, beef, or pork. Or dice and cook it in soup—either a creamed version or a mixed vegetable in clear broth with beef.

Celtuce

Grow celtuce, a cultivated variety of lettuce, the same as celery. Allow 1½ square feet of growing space for each plant.

The big difference between head lettuce and celtuce is that you want celtuce to go to seed—the thickened stem that shoots up from the "lettuce" base is what you are after. You can use the leaves of the young plant as lettuce or as boiled greens. Use the heart of the stem in all the ways you would in preparing celery. Harvest when the stalk is about an inch thick at the base. It remains flavorful until the flower buds. Catalog source: (5).

Chayote

This member of the gourd family (see chart on page 103) is native to Mexico and Central America. As a fresh fruit it appears in the specialty produce markets of the U.S. in late fall and winter as chayote (chy-*oh*-tee) or vegetable pear. It's also known as the one-seeded cucumber, and the Creoles call it merliton.

Chayote grows as a perennial, and as an evergreen some years in southern California. In mild-winter areas frost kills the tops each winter, but the vine renews itself each spring.

This fast-growing vine will cover a pergola, wall, or a 10- to 15-foot section of a fence with large, lobed leaves by midsummer.

Flowering begins when the days shorten in late summer. Harvest starts about a month after flowering and continues until the vine is stopped by frost. A strong healthy vine in a favorable climate will produce as many as 100 fruits.

The fruit will weigh ½ to 1 pound. It's somewhat pear shaped and furrowed. Color varies from very light to dark green.

The whole fruit is used as "seed." Plant it with the large end sloping downward into the soil, and with the small end slightly exposed.

If you know someone who grows chayote, or if you buy the fresh fruit when it's available in produce markets, you'll get a head start. Just store it in a cool place until the soil warms up in the spring, then plant. If, during the storage period, the fruits send out long shoots, cut them back to 2 inches when you plant.

You can prepare chayote in as many ways as squash, and more. Dice them, then steam until tender; bake and stuff them; cook them, then marinate and use in salads; pickle them—even candy them.

Chayote has a mild flavor and is used primarily in Mexican cooking.

Chinese Cabbage—Celery Cabbage

The name Chinese cabbage covers a number of "greens" that differ in character. All are cool-weather crops and bolt to seed during the long days of late spring and summer. Grow this vegetable as a fall and early winter crop.

How to grow. Sow seeds thinly and later thin to stand 18 inches apart in rows 24 to 30 inches apart. Chinese cabbage takes about 75 to 85 days to grow from seed to harvest.

Time to sow seeds in place (for dates, see Cabbage, page 82)

Varieties. 'Wong Bok' (85 days). This is the Chinese cabbage most frequently available at supermarkets. Heads are about 10 inches tall, 6 inches wide, and completely blanched.

'Early Hybrid "G" Chinese Cabbage' (50 to 60 days) does not bolt quickly to seed in early plantings. May be grown as an early spring crop, as well as fall.

'Burpee Hybrid' (Wong Bok type). Heads are round, 13 inches tall, and 8 inches thick.

'Michihli' (75 days). An improved form of Chihli. Forms a tall, 18-inch, tapering head 3 to 4 inches thick, with dark green wrapper leaves and well-blanched inner leaves.

'Pac-Choy'. Nonheading type. One of the most popular of the oriental vegetables. Widely grown in Hawaii as one of the "Spoon Cabbages." These resemble Swiss chard (without heavy stalks) in growth habit.

Serving ideas. This pale whitish-green cabbage is favored for soups, sukiyakis, and stir-fry medleys. It is also well suited to western dishes. Shred it for a cab-

Chinese cabbage.

Chives, with their lavender flowers, are ornamental as well as flavorful.

Collards are a member of the cabbage family with a long and distinguished history

bage slaw with fresh pineapple and a sour cream dressing. Boil wedges to accompany corned beef or other *pot-au-feu*-type dishes. Shred and toss it with macadamia nuts and avocado chunks, bound in a tart creamy dressing. Or shred and butter-steam it to accompany roast pork or duck. Use the broad leaves for cabbage rolls, stuffed with a minced pork and water chestnut filling.

Chives

Chives have been used for ages. In 812, Emperor Charlemagne included them on the list of herbs to be grown in his garden. Today, no vegetable gardener would refuse to give them room.

This hardy perennial is willing to be clipped almost continuously. If not clipped, chives produce pompoms of lavender flower heads above their grasslike hollow leaves every spring. A half-dozen pots will supply enough snippings for year-round use. Chives will take kitchen window-sill treatment. Frozen chopped chives are almost as good as fresh. Clumps of chives add a gay touch to the flower border.

How to grow. Buy plants for an easy way to a quick harvest. Small clumps spread rapidly. Or grow from seeds started in small pots. Chives grow best in rich moist soil in full sun, but will tolerate filtered shade.

How to use. Use scissors to snip these fine, grasslike blades with delicate onion flavor for salads, dips, and various fish, chicken, and meat dishes. Chive butter lends a delightful aroma and succulence to steaks and broiled seafood. It is a fine spread for hot egg bread or sourdough rye, as well.

Collards

This perennial is one of the oldest members of the cabbage family. Vegetable historians claim that it has been used for food for more than 4,000 years and cultivated in its present form for 2,000 years. European writers described it in the 1st, 3rd, and 4th centuries, and early American gardens sported it by 1669.

The South has considered collards a favorite for generations, but they adapt widely and are finding their way into more and more gardens. Unlike their close relative, kale, collards withstand hot summer weather and will take much more cold than cabbage.

How to grow. Collards have the same fertilizing and water requirements as cabbage. There are several planting methods: (1) In spring, sow seed or set out plants to stand 10 to 15 inches apart. (2) Set plants close, 5 to 7 inches apart, to dwarf them to small bunchy plants. Harvest leaves as needed. (3) In summer plantings, sow seed thinly and let the seedlings grow until they are large enough for greens, then harvest them to give the normal distance between plants.

Time to sow seeds in place (for dates, see Cabbage, page 82).

Varieties. 'Georgia' (southern, Creole; matures in 70 to 80 days). Old standard variety. Plants are 24 to 30 inches tall, with very broad, slightly crumpled, medium- to blue-green leaves.

'Louisiana Sweet' (85 days). Larger leaf area than 'Georgia'. Thick tender leaves are an appealing color.

'Vates' (75 days). Low growing, broad, and spreading. Thick, very broad-bladed, grassy green leaves.

'Morris Heading' (83 days). Leaves are broad and wavy, forming a moderately tight head that's good for winter planting.

Serving ideas. Pick the leaves when they're young and have small midribs. Chop them finely and boil in salted water until tender; serve them dressed with butter or hot bacon drippings. Collards get along well with ham and pork and often are cooked with a ham hock or salt pork. Use them in a hearty pea soup seasoned with green pepper, onion, and ham bone.

Cowpeas—Southern Table Peas

Cowpeas originally came from Middle Asia, but it spread to Asia Minor and Africa before the slave traders brought it to the warm climates of the West Indies, where it became an important food.

Cowpeas have a more distinctive flavor than garden peas. They require heat —warm days and warm nights—and are damaged by the slightest frosts.

When to plant. Plant when the soil is warmed up. Cowpeas germinate better in warm soil. Sow seed ½ to 1 inch deep— 5 to 8 seeds per foot of row. Thin to 3 to 4 inches between plants. Leave 24 to 36 inches between rows. Go easy on nitrogen fertilizer—all you really need is a side dressing of 5-10-10 fertilizer at 3 pounds per 100 feet of row after the plants are up.

You can pick cowpeas in the green-shell stage, when the seeds are fully developed but not yet hard, as is the tradition; or you can let them ripen and store them as dried peas.

Varieties. Several mail-order seed companies offer varieties of the various types of cowpeas.

Recommended varieties:

'Brown Sugar Crowder'. Large green peas mature in 85 to 90 days.

'Mississippi Silver'. A crowder type. Widely adapted.

'Purple Hull Pink Eye'. When young, the peas are white with a small pink eye.

'Early Ramshorn Black Eye'. You'll get green peas in 60 days. Resistant to wilt and nematodes.

Cowpeas—a warm-weather vegetable with a distinctive flavor.

Blackeyed peas

Corn

The word "corn" has meant many things—originally, any hard particle, grain, sand, or salt. "Corned" beef is so named because it is cured with salt. Both wheat and barley were called corn in the Old World. Maize, the main cereal of the New World, was first known as "Indian corn," and later just as "corn."

Corn supported the early civilizations of the Americas. Fossils show that corn was grown in North America as early as 4,000 years ago. After America was discovered, corn spread rapidly throughout the Old World.

How to grow. Plant seed 2 inches deep, 4 to 6 seeds per foot, in rows 30 to 36 inches apart. Thin to 10 to 14 inches between plants. Plant early, midseason, and late varieties or make successive plantings every 2 or 3 weeks for a continuous supply of sweet corn through summer and into the fall.

Can you get more corn per foot of space? A number of our gardeners argued about the need to space corn 10 to 14 inches in the row and 30 to 36 inches between rows.

"More home garden corn plantings are ruined by overcrowding than by any other factor. When seedlings are up, everyone hates to pull them out and throw them away. Actually, too many seedlings in a row act just like weeds."

"The smaller-growing early varieties might be spaced 8 inches apart in rows 30 inches apart, but with the later varieties such as 'Golden Cross Bantam', I like to get them spaced out to a good 12 to 15 inches for good ear production."

"If you overspace corn, you generally are compensated by more usable ears and some sucker production."

How much fertilizer and when? This is the schedule that most of our specialists approved:

"At planting time, fertilize in bands on both sides of the seed row, 2 inches from seed in the furrow and an inch deeper than seed level. Use 3 pounds of 5-10-10 (in each band) per 100 feet of row. When the corn is 8 inches high, sidedress it with the same amount. Repeat when it's knee-high (18 inches)."

Watering. It's water all the way for corn. Here's what the corn specialists said:

"Sweet corn makes very rapid growth during the time when the crop is maturing. It is particularly important to keep the plants well watered during this time. The water need is greater from tasseling time to picking time."

"In very hot and dry weather, rolling of the leaves may occur in midday even when soil moisture is adequate. Plants will transpire water faster than the roots will absorb water. But if the leaves roll, check the soil for moisture."

Do's and don'ts. Corn is pollinated by wind. Plant in short blocks of 3 to 4 rows rather than a single row.

Don't worry about the suckers; the number varies according to the variety. Contrary to popular belief, they do not take strength from the main stalks. Tests have shown that removing suckers may reduce the yields.

In most areas, corn earworms will damage your corn unless you take steps to stop them. See page 58 for ways to control these insects.

Ears with tight husks and a good tip cover are safer from corn-earworm damage. They do not prevent the worms from entering, but they do reduce the damage. The list of varieties that follows mentions those with tight husks.

Tight husks and good tip cover have another advantage. A corn specialist reports: "We have a terrible time with birds eating the kernels on the tip of the ear. The damage is worse on ears with loose husks. And such damage makes the ornamental Indian corn worthless. We solved the problem by slipping a paper bag over each ear after it was pollinated."

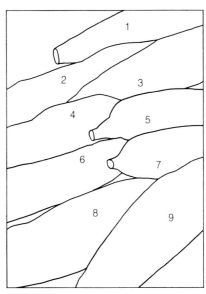

1. 'Purple Husk', **2.** An inferior early variety, **3.** 'Silver Queen', **4.** Indian corn. **5.** Indian corn, **6.** Yellow hybrid, **7.** Popcorn, **8.** 'Country Gentleman', **9.** Indian corn.

Time to sow seeds in place

Zone/South		Zone/North		Zone/West	
1	1/1-2/28	**5**	4/20-6/15	**6, 8, 13**	5/20-6/20
2	1/30-3/30	**6**	5/1-6/15	**9**	6/1-6/30
3	3/1-4/30	**7**	5/20-6/30	**10**	6/1-6/30
4	3/15-7/20	**8**	5/20-6/30	**12**	5/20-6/10
5	4/1-7/5	**9**	6/1-6/30	**14**	1/1-5/30
6	4/15-6/30	**10**	6/1-6/30	**15, 21**	2/1-7/30
7	5/20-6/30	**11**	5/20-6/15	**16, 17**	5/15-6/15
13	5/20-6/30			**18**	4/1-7/30
				19	4/1-7/30
				20	1/1-7/30
				22	3/1-7/30

Varieties. At least once, you deserve to experience the "bi-colors," with their mixture of white and yellow kernels. The 'Xtra Sweet' varieties contain more sugar than the standard varieties, and their sugar changes to starch slowly.

In every trial of varieties, the variety 'Silver Queen' has been rated "the highest quality corn ever developed."

Corn, ready for the pot.

On the following chart, (R) indicates resistance to bacterial wilt. Tight-husked varieties are indicated by (T.H.).

The number of days to maturity varies by the total amount of heat the corn receives. Varieties listed as 65 days may take 80 or 90 when planted early. Corn does not grow until the weather warms. The same variety will come close to its cataloged 65 days if planted a month later.

When planting for a succession of harvests, consider the effect of cool spring weather. Let the height of the first planting set the date for the second.

Variety	Zone	Color	Days	Ear Length	Rows Per Ear	Height	—
Early Sunglow	W	Y	63	7	10-12	4-6	—
Royal Crest	W	Y	64	6½-7½	12	5½	—
Tokay Sugar	W	W	65	6-7	8-12	6	—
Earliking	W/N	Y	66	7-8	12	5½	—
Spring Gold	W/N	Y	67	7	12-16	5-6	T.H.
Golden Beauty	N/S	Y	67	6-7½	14	5½-6	R.
Marcross Golden Belle	N	Y	69	6½-8	12-14	6	R.
Sugar & Gold	W/N	Bl	70	6-6½	8-10	4-6	—
Early Xtra Sweet	W	Y	71	7-9	12-16	4-6	—
Golden Security	S	Y	75	8-8½	14-16	8	T.H.
Gold Cup	N/S	Y	77	7½	14-16	6½	—
Butter & Sugar	W/N	Bl	78	6½-7½	12-14	6	—
Seneca Chief	N/S	Y	80	8-8½	14	6-7	T.H.
Merit	S	Y	82	5	18	6	—
Jubilee	W	Y	84	8½-9	18-20	7-7½	—
NK 199	W	Y	84	8½-9	18-20	7½-8	—
Golden Cross Bantam	W/N/S	Y	85	7½-8½	10-14	6-7	R.
Illini Extra Sweet	W	Y	85	8	14-18	4-6	—
Iochief	W/N	Y	85	9-10	14-18	6½	R.
Aristogold Bantam Evergreen	S	Y	90	9-10	16-18	7-8	R.
Golden Queen	S	Y	93	8-9	14-16	9	—
Silver Queen	W/N/S	W	96	8-9	14-16	7-8	R.

Corn Salad Or Lamb's Lettuce Or Fetticus

The only reason why this is called "corn" salad is that in Europe it frequently sprouts in the fall in harvested corn fields. In this country it comes from the garden when the weather is too cold for lettuce.

This bland-flavored vegetable goes well in salads with strong-flavored leaves such as mustard and endive. Dress the green salad with oil and vinegar. Use corn salad alone as a salad base for a medley of cooked vegetables: celery root, beets, green beans, garbanzos, and red peppers.

How to grow. Grow the same as lettuce. Plant rows 12 to 18 inches apart; sow seeds 5 to 6 inches apart in the row.

When to plant. Try for a winter crop by planting later than lettuce in the fall. See "Lettuce."

Cress

Four kinds of cress are cultivated in gardens, and numerous cresses grow wild. These generally are gathered in the spring and used as a substitute for water-cress. Common names for these are lamb's cress, lady's smock, meadow cress, marsh cress, Pennsylvania bitter cress, and penny cress. The four cultivated kinds are:

Garden cress or pepper grass. The variety 'Fine Curled', 'Curled', or Burpee's 'Curlycress' has the look of parsley. It is a fast-growing annual that is used in the sprout stage, when leaves form in 7 to 10 days, and in all stages up to maturity in 6 weeks. It goes quickly to flower in the long days of summer.

Plant early in the season in rows 8 to 12 inches apart, and use the thinnings. Make successive sowings in spring and again in fall. Keep the soil moist and feed frequently but lightly.

Upland cress. This watercress-like cress makes a dense growth 5 to 6 inches high and 10 to 12 inches wide. Sow seed in rows 12 to 14 inches apart. Thin to 4 to 8 inches apart, and use the thinnings. The young tender tips will be ready in about 7 weeks. Upland cress will withstand fall frosts. Requires moist soil.

Winter cress or Belle Island cress. This hardy biennial survives severe winters. Sow in late summer, and use in winter and summer, before seed stalks develop.

Watercress. This hardy aquatic perennial has been grown as a food and a medicine for 2000 years. Its health-giving qualities, extolled by the ancients, are recognized by modern medicine as well. The earliest explorers brought the seed from Europe. Today, you can find it in many areas, wherever there are springs and small, slow-running streams.

You can grow watercress from either seed or cuttings. You can even take cuttings from the watercress you buy at the market. Stick them in sand or in a planter mix in a pot. Set them in a tub of water. Sow the seed, which is very small, in small containers; transplant when the plants are 2 or 3 inches tall. If you can supply enough water to keep the soil continuously moist—even by a drip method—you can grow watercress in a cold frame, planter box, or trench.

If you have a small stream or spring that's suitable for growing watercress, send 10¢ for the detailed information contained in *Commercial Growing of Watercress* (Farmers Bulletin No. 2233) to Superintendent of Documents, Washington, D.C. 20402.

How to serve. Cress is a spicy, fresh addition to salads. Mingle the sprigs with raw mushrooms, sliced and marinated in a vinaigrette for a first-course salad plate. Mix watercress sprigs with chunks of chicken, toasted almonds, and seedless grapes in a sour cream dressing for a luncheon salad. Line butter lettuce with watercress sprigs and dress with oil and vinegar to serve with the cheese course. Pair cress with sliced hearts of palm and crab or shrimp for a luncheon salad plate.

In sandwiches, watercress lends a sprightly bite. Tuck sprigs into sliced chicken and tomato sandwiches. Or layer with sliced avocado and bacon on toasted egg bread.

Cress also goes well in a creamy chicken broth. Or drop shredded leaves into a smooth potato and onion soup. As a garnish, the fresh, deep green color and spicy undertones of cress enhance a variety of entree platters.

A lush patch of watercress.

Cucumber

This vegetable probably came from India, originally. Vegetable historians do know that it was introduced into China around 200 B.C. In 1535, the French found the Indians growing cucumbers in what is now Montreal.

Because of its short growing season (55 to 60 days from seed to picking size) the cucumber can find the warm slice of climate it needs almost everywhere. It does well with less heat than melons require.

Time to sow seeds in place (sow seeds indoors 4 weeks earlier)

Zone/South		Zone/North		Zone/West	
1	1/1-2/28	**5**	4/15-5/15, 7/1-8/15	**6, 8, 13**	5/20-7/10
2	1/15-3/30	**6**	4/20-6/10	**9**	6/1-7/5
3	2/20-4/15	**7**	5/10-6/15	**10**	—
4	3/15-4/30	**8**	5/15-6/30	**12**	5/20-6/10
5	4/1-5/30	**9**	6/1-7/5	**14**	2/1-5/30
6	4/15-5/15	**10**	—	**15, 21**	3/1-6/30
7	5/15-6/15	**11**	5/2-6/1	**16, 17**	5/20-7/10
13	5/20-7/15			**18**	4/1-6/30
				19	1/20-6/30
				20	5/15-7/15
				22	4/1-6/30

Immature cucumber with bloom still attached.

Above: 'Patio Pik'. Above right: Armenian cucumbers grow straight when trained on a trellis. Below: A burpless variety.

How to grow. Sow the seeds 1 inch deep, 3 to 5 seeds to 1 foot of row. Thin to 12 inches between plants. The distance between rows should be 48 to 72 inches if you are growing the standard vining varieties. The newer, more compact bush varieties take up less space, and can be placed closer together. If you're growing the plants in hills, sow 9 to 12 seeds in each hill. Then, when the plants are up, thin to 4 or 6, and finally to 2 or 3 per hill. Space hills 24 to 36 inches apart in rows 48 to 72 inches apart.

Where the growing season is short, start seed indoors in peat pots 4 to 6 weeks before it's time to set out transplants (see "Transplants," page 52). Be careful when transplanting, since any root damage will affect future growth. When setting out transplants, cover plants with hot caps or plastic to increase the temperature and protect them from frost.

Fertilizing and watering. Cucumbers respond to generous amounts of organic matter in the soil. For special treatment, dig the planting furrow 2 feet deep and fill the first foot or so with manure mixed with peat moss, compost, sawdust, or other organic material. Fill the rest of the furrow with soil, peat moss, and 5-10-10 fertilizer at the rate of 2 pounds to 50 feet of row.

Since the roots will grow to a depth of 3 feet in normal soil, water slowly and deeply. If the plant is under stress from lack of moisture at any time, it just stops growing; however, it will pick up again when it receives moisture. It is normal for leaves of cucumbers to wilt in the middle of the day during hot spells, but check the soil for moisture at the below-surface levels.

When space is limited. If you train your cucumbers on a trellis, they will take very little ground space and you will harvest more attractive fruits and fewer culls. Cucumbers such as "Burpee Hybrid," which are curved when grown on the ground, grow almost straight when trained on a trellis.

When space is limited, consider the midget varieties. They can be grown on the ground, in tubs and boxes, or in hanging baskets. Two such varieties are:

'Tiny Dill Duke' (55 days). Vines spread only 2 feet. Produces near finger-length cukes. University of New Hampshire development.

'Patio Pik' (60 days). The vine is very dwarf, spreading only 18 to 24 inches. Pick small size for dills, a larger size for slicing. Grows up to 7 inches long.

Don't worry that the first early flowers fail to set fruit. The male flowers open first; then, about a week later, you'll see flowers with baby cucumbers

When you grow and preserve "picklers," the harvest extends through the year.

at their bases (see photograph, page 93). The male flowers supply the pollen, which insects transfer to the female flowers.

If this delayed setting worries you, try one of the new all-female (gynoecious) hybrids. Since they set fruit with the first blossoms, they bear fruit closer to the base of the plant.

As all fruits reach usable size, pick them from the vines. This can't be over-emphasized—even a few fruit left to mature on the plant will completely stop the set of new fruit. If you can't keep up and want the fruit to keep coming, invite your neighbors to share your harvest.

Varieties. Depending on the locality, disease resistance can be an important factor in growing cucumbers. Disease resistance or tolerance is indicated as follows: Scab (S), Mosaic (M), Downy Mildew (DM), Powdery Mildew (PM), and Anthracnose (A). Gynoecious hybrids (Gyn.) are all or nearly all female.

'Gemini Hybrid'. (Gyn.), (DM), (M), (PM), (A), (S).

'Burpee Hybrid'. (M), (DM).

'Ashley'. Clemson. (DM).

'Marketer'. (DM), (M).

'Spartan Valor'. (Gyn.), (M), (S).

'Saticoy Hybrid'. (M), (D).

'Sweet Slice'. (M).

'Surecrop' (58 days). All-America Selection.

'Victory' (60 days). All-America Selection.

'Saladin' (55 days). All-America Selection.

'Liberty' (54 days). All-America Selection.

·'Marketmore'. Cornell. (S), (M).

'Triumph Hybrid'. All-America Selection. (DM), (M).

'Cherokee Hybrid'. Clemson. (Gyn.), (DM), (M), (PM), (A).

'Poinsett'. (DM), (PM), (A).

'Meridian'. Cornell. (S), (M).

Picklers. Many varieties are available. These have the advantage of disease resistance:

'Pioneer'. (Gyn.), (S), (M), (DM), (PM).

'SMR 58'. (S), (M).

'SMR 18'. (S), (M).

'Ohio MR 17'. (M).

Many kinds. Cucumbers come in a wide variety of shapes and colors. There's a white one—'White Wonder' (4), (26). The 'Lemon Cucumber' is the size and shape of a lemon; at maturity it turns a lemon yellow and then a golden yellow. This old-timer is easy to grow, always sweet, and as burpless as any we have grown (5), (12), (13), (16), (19), (27).

The Armenian cucumber is favored by all who have grown it and is excellent for growing on a trellis.

'Burpless Hybrid' (60 days) is an excellent producer of 8- to 10-inch-long fruits, 30 to 40 per plant. Mild and nearly seedless.

Serving ideas. This is a popular salad and pickle vegetable. Slice and serve cucumbers in a white vinegar/sugar/dill bath for a Scandinavian "wilted" salad; serve sliced cucumbers in a yogurt and mint dressing for a Near Eastern meal; or mix fresh slices with sour cream and chopped parsley.

Wild dandelion

Dandelion

Dandelion means "tooth of the lion," a name that comes from this green's jagged, irregular leaves. Native to Europe and Asia, its seeds have traveled far and wide.

As a garden vegetable it tops all other vegetables and fruits in iron and vitamin A.

How to grow. Sow seed and transplant, or seed in place in rows 12 to 16 inches apart. Thin to stand about 12 inches in the row. A good supply of moisture and fertilizer encourages fast growth, which this plant needs to become a quality product.

When to plant. Plant it at the same time as lettuce for an early crop, or seed in July through August for a fall crop or a very early spring crop the following year. Since dandelion is a perennial, if it is allowed to develop and store food all season it will experience a rush of new growth the following spring.

You can blanch dandelion tops by tying up leaves, or by covering the tops with any light-concealing material. The popular variety is 'Improved Thick Leaved'.

Serving ideas. The young leaves fresh from the garden are tenderest and best. Try them in salads (without stalks) tossed in a vinaigrette dressing, or dress the leaves with hot bacon drippings, vinegar, and crumbled bacon crisps.

Cook the leaves quickly with a dash of olive oil and serve Greek style, with lemon wedges and oregano as an accompaniment to fish. For an Italian dish, mix the boiled leaves with hot spaghetti and toss with olive oil and freshly shredded Parmesan cheese.

Edible-Podded Sugar Peas (Snow Peas)

'Dwarf Gray Sugar' (63 days) is a low grower (24 inches) that can be grown without staking. The tall growers are 'Mammoth Melting Sugar' (72 days) and 'Burpee Sweet Pod' (68 days). Pick them when they're very young, just as the peas start to form. If you miss that stage, you can shell and eat the peas, but the pods will be too tough to eat.

Time to sow seeds in place (for dates, see Peas, page 117).

Harvesting. Repeated pickings, taking only the plump lower pods from the plant, will give the best yield. You can do a better job of picking if you grow the

Edible-podded sugar peas (snow peas)

Two unusual eggplant varieties:
Above: Japanese eggplant. Above right:
Dwarf golden eggplant.

peas on a trellis. Harvest them in the cool of the morning rather than in the heat of the afternoon. Rinse the peas in cool water as soon as possible after picking, and refrigerate for later use.

Eggplant

A 5th-century Chinese book contains one of the oldest references to eggplant. A black dye was made from the plant, and ladies of fashion used it to stain their teeth—which, when polished, gleamed like metal.

Wild eggplant grows in India, and it was first cultivated there. Then the Arabs took it to Spain, the Spaniards took it to the Americas, and the Persians took it to Africa.

The eggplants cultivated in various European countries in the 16th and 17th centuries varied greatly in shape and color. Apparently, the first known of these belong to what is now considered an ornamental class; the fruit resembles an egg. Later, the varying shapes were described as long, pear shaped, oblong, round, or spherical, and the colors were reported to be purple, yellow, white, ash-colored, and variegated. By 1806, both purple and white ornamentals were seen growing in American gardens.

Today, only the large-fruited varieties are grown on a commercial scale. Florida, Mexico, and California supply the markets in the winter and spring months; New Jersey, Ohio, Colorado, Michigan, Illinois, Missouri, New York, and Texas make their contributions in September and October.

Time to sow seeds in place (sow seed indoors 7-10 weeks earlier)

Zone/South		Zone/North		Zone/West	
1	4/20-5/31	**5**	4/20-5/31	**6, 8, 13**	5/20-6/15
2	5/1-6/15	**6**	5/1-6/15	**9**	6/1-6/20
3	5/15-6/15	**7**	5/15-6/15	**10**	—
4	5/20-6/20	**8**	5/20-6/20	**12**	—
5	6/1-6/20	**9**	6/1-6/20	**14**	2/1-5/30. 8/1-8/30
6	—	**10**	—	**15, 21**	3/1-4/30
7	—	**11**	5/20-6/1	**16, 17**	—
13	5/20-6/15			**18**	5/1-6/5
				19	2/20-5/15
				20	4/20-6/10
				22	4/1-5/30

Eggplant needs very high heat. It thrives best at 78° during the day and 68° at night. The large-fruited kinds are more demanding than varieties with smaller fruits. Select early varieties where summers are short.

Varieties. More than 30 varieties are available. Some of the most popular ones recommended in the northern and western growing regions are: 'Black Beauty' (75 to 80 days to maturity). This is the most frequently recommended large-fruited variety. However, the hybrids such as 'Black Magic' and 'Burpee Hybrid' are favored for their earliness, vigor, and disease resistance. They grow taller than 'Black Beauty' and hold their fruit well off the ground. 'Jersey King Hybrid' produces elongated cylindrical fruits. 'Early Beauty Hybrid' is a compact grower, with short oval fruits that resemble 'New Hampshire Hybrid'. 'Dusky' is an early variety (55-60 days) favored for its high-quality medium-sized fruits. 'Black Bell' (60 days) is an excellent new variety. 'Icheban' is an Oriental variety with long (12 inch), slender fruit.

The standard large-fruited varieties for the southern states are 'Black Beauty', 'Florida High Bush', 'Florida Market', and 'Florida Meyer'. The Florida varieties are taller-growing than 'Black Beauty', 30 to 36 inches, and hold their fruit well off the ground. All the above are in the 80 to 90 days-to-maturity range. The variety 'Hastings Purple Thornless' produces 4 to 8 large purple fruits on a 28- to 32-inch bush. Some of the old-fashioned and unusual varieties you'll find listed in various catalogs (see page 140) are:

'Golden Yellow' (19) and 'Golden Egg'. Highly ornamental. Plants have produced more than 20 lemon-sized eggs per plant.

'Apple Green'. (9) Fruits are non-acid, don't require peeling.

'White Beauty' (9) and 'White Italian'. Medium-sized fruits. Delicate flavor.

'Morden Midget'. (9) (21) Medium-sized, deep purple fruits grow on sturdy, small bushy plants. Developed at Morden, Canada, Experiment Station.

How to grow. Buy plants or start seed indoors 6 to 9 weeks before it's time to set out transplants. (See transplanting procedure, page 52.) Set plants 18 inches apart in rows 36 inches apart. The fruits will be ready to harvest in 75 to 95 days after setting out the transplants.

Eggplant is more susceptible to low-temperature injury—especially that caused by cold nights—than tomatoes are. Don't set out plants until the daily temperatures are in the 70° range. Plants that fail to grow because of cool weather become hardened and stunted. Once stunted, they seldom make the rapid growth needed to produce quality fruit. Apply a side-dressing of fertilizer a month after planting, and repeat in a month.

Mistakes beginners make. Setting out plants before the weather is warm. Failing to protect against cold by using hot caps or plastic covers. Failing to protect young plants against damage by flea beetles and Colorado potato beetles. See "Pests and Controls," page 58.

Special handling. The eggplant is well adapted to container growing. We have grown half a dozen varieties in 5-gallon containers without a single failure. Using one of the synthetic soil mixes in containers is good insurance against the diseases that plague eggplant in some areas. (See page 36.) In containers,

Chicory blossoms

the varieties with medium- to small-sized fruits carried high on the plant are more interesting than the lower-growing, heavy-fruited varieties.

Where summers are cool, put containers in the hot spots around the house —for example, where heat is reflected from a south wall.

Harvest. For best eating quality, pick fruits when they're young—from 1/3 to 2/3 their normal mature size. Good fruit has a high gloss. One test for maturity is to push on the side of the fruit with the ball of the thumb. If the indentation does not spring back, the fruit is slightly mature. Fruits in which seeds have turned brown are past the eating stage. The stem is woody, so harvest with pruning shears.

Serving ideas. Don't decide that you don't like eggplant until you have tried these recipes.

France, Italy, Greece, and the Near East have wonderful ways with eggplant. Prepare it in a southern French baked vegetable casserole called *ratatouille*, or simmer spears, Greek style, in a court bouillon.

For a Near Eastern salad, bake a whole eggplant. Place the whole eggplant in a shallow pan and bake it in a 375° oven for 1 hour or until tender. Place it under cold water and peel off the skin. Dice and mix with chopped green onions, tomatoes, garlic, and oil and vinegar. Serve cold on Romaine leaves.

Eggplant soaks up considerable oil or butter when fried. If you don't want to fry it in oil, an easy way is to cut it into ¾-inch-thick slices, lay these slices in a lightly oiled baking pan, and bake in a 425° oven for 30 minutes, turning several times.

Endive, Chicory, Escarole

You can buy these lacy, slightly bitter greens at the market under the names "chicory" or "endive"—they are sold as both. But when you want to plant this vegetable, buy endive *(Cichorium endivia).* Escarole is a broad-leafed form of endive.

If you want to try your hand at producing the blanched, tubular French or Belgian endive, buy seeds of Witloof chicory *(Cichorium itybus)* (see description below).

Grow endive like lettuce. However, it is at its best when grown for fall or winter harvest.

The finely cut type is represented by the varieties 'Green Curled', 'Pancalier', and 'Ruffec'.

The less frilled, broad-leaved type, often called "escarole," is cataloged as 'Full Heart Batavian' and 'Florida Deep Hearted'.

Both types are best for salads when blanched. Draw the outer leaves together and tie them with a string. In 2 to 3 weeks, the blanching should be complete.

How to serve. Wash and chill until crisp. Tear into bite-sized pieces and mix with an oil and vinegar dressing. Embellish with blue cheese and garlic croutons.

Try a Greek country salad: a medley of tomato wedges, sliced cucumbers, black olives, anchovy fillets, feta cheese, and bite-sized pieces of endive. Or mix endive in an Italian salad of sliced green or red peppers, artichoke hearts, sliced eggs, sardines, Romaine, and an oil and vinegar dressing with shredded Parmesan cheese. The French favor chicory and hot sausage in a unique wilted salad. The slightly bitter taste of endive may take a little getting used to—don't be surprised with the first bite.

How to grow Witloof chicory or French endive or Belgian endive. Sow seeds in early summer. Seeds require 5 months to produce the roots, which are grown like parsnips. Do not plant too early. A plant that goes to seed is useless for the next step, called forcing. Dig the roots in the fall and cut off the tops 2 inches above the crown to prevent injury to crown buds. Store the roots in a cool place and force them at room temperatures of 60° to 70°F., as follows:

Cut the tip of the root so that is is uniform in length, about 6 to 9 inches. Set roots in an upright position in a trench or box, with the crown up. Fill the space between the roots with soil. After thoroughly wetting the soil, cover the entire vegetable, root and crown, with sand to a depth of 6 to 8 inches. Keep the soil moist. The sand keeps the heads compact and excludes light, causing blanching. 3 to 4 weeks are required to produce good heads weighing 2 to 3 ounces and measuring 4 to 6 inches tall. Medium-sized roots (1 to 1¾ inches in diameter) produce the largest yield. Small roots produce low yields; large roots produce compound heads.

Varieties. 'Large-Rooted Madgeburg'. Grows about 15 inches tall with upright, dandelionlike foliage. Roots are 12 to 14 inches long. Young tender leaves can be harvested for greens at about 65 days; roots are mature at about 120 days.

'Cicoria Catalogna' or 'Radichetta' (65 days to harvest leaves). Leaves are toothed and curled. Used for early greens. The flower shoots are edible, with a faint asparagus flavor.

'Cicoria San Pasquale' (70 days to harvest leaves). Light green leaves are broader than Madgeburg; used for greens.

Above: Florence fennel
Left: Endive

Florence Fennel—Finocchio

Florence fennel was described as Azorian Dwarf or Finocchio in 1778. It was planted in American gardens around 1800. Florence fennel is a variety of the herb fennel and is grown for its bulblike base that's formed by overlapping leafstalks. Sow seed indoors in peat pots and set out in early spring, 8 to 12 inches apart in rows 24 inches apart. Give it a well-fertilized soil and plenty of water. As the plants develop thickened bases, pull up soil to cover and blanch them.

Cool weather is almost essential for successful growth. Where spring is short and summers are hot, sow seed in summer for a fall crop.

You can use the leaves in the same ways as you'd use common fennel. In fact, some seed catalogs list this variety as common fennel. In produce markets you may find Florence fennel labeled "anise."

Serving ideas. This is an important vegetable in Italian cooking, and it has many uses. You can braise or steam the stalks and treat them in all the ways appropriate to celery. Eat the bulbous base raw, or briefly blanch and chill it for a flavorful addition to salads. Braised fennel goes well with pasta or risotto dishes.

Garden Huckleberry

If you happen to read that "this is the cultivated form of the poisonous black nightshade," change "cultivated" to "edible" and you'll be in for a treat. This relative of the potato and eggplant grows to about 2½ feet.

Don't use the fruits of the garden huckleberry *(Solanum nigrum)* until they turn thoroughly black. Light frosts don't harm them; in fact, they improve the flavor. The fruits sometimes have a bitter taste which can be neutralized by parboiling them for 10 minutes in water containing a pinch of baking soda. When combined with lemons, apples, or grapes, garden huckleberry makes excellent jellies and preserves. Catalog sources are: (4), (9), (12), (16), (20), (26), (27).

Garlic

Two types of garlic are available: the type you buy at the market—a bulb containing about 10 small cloves—and 'Elephant Garlic', which is about 6 times larger and may weigh as much as a pound. 'Elephant Garlic' has a slightly milder flavor than the standard garlic.

Both are grown in the same way.

In all but the coldest areas, set out cloves in the fall an inch deep, 2 to 4 inches apart in rows 12 to 18 inches apart. Harvest when the tops fall over; braid into strings or tie in bunches and hang in a cool dry place.

Sources for 'Elephant Garlic' are catalogs (4) and (19).

Serving ideas. This potent bulb is indispensable in many different cuisines. The aromatic cloves lend pungency to a range of dishes.

Mince garlic and add to melted butter as a sauce for lobster, snails, mushrooms, broccoli, and green beans, and as a spread for French bread. Brown nuggets of garlic in butter as a finish on veal or pork scallopini or chicken breasts. Mince garlic for meatballs and slow-cooking meat sauce. Sliver garlic to poke into lamb or beef roasts and lamb shanks.

Steep a garlic clove in red or white wine vinegar to imbue it with flavor for salad dressings.

Use garlic in the Provencal mayonnaise called *Aioli* and the Greek almond mayonnaise called *Skordalia.* Include it in the Spanish cold gazpacho soups and the hot garlic soups on which crusty bread and poached eggs are floated.

Gourds

Three different circumstances led us to include gourds in this book.

First, our gardeners began asking for identification of a strange vegetable creation that appeared in their supposedly honest vegetable patches.

Second, more and more "edible" gourds are finding their way into vegetable seed catalogs.

Third, we received letters from irate gardeners who claimed that we were misleading gardeners by telling them not to worry about cucumbers crossing with melons.

These developments convinced us that we needed a botanist to determine where the *edible* and *inedible* varieties belonged in the gourd family, and to set us straight about crossing.

The chart on the opposite page is the result. In some ways it's quite shocking—never again will we be quite so confident about the common names of squash and pumpkin as before we read the chart.

If you look down the "genus" column in the chart, you will come upon *Lagenaria* and its one species, *siceraria.* These are the larger gourds, often listed in seed catalogs as such separate varieties as bottle, dipper, and 'Hercules Club'. In many regions of the world, all domestic utensils were made of lagenarias

Garden huckleberry.

Almost everyone's favorite: garlic.

before pottery was invented. Those gourds were made into bottles, bowls, ladles, spoons, churns, and many types of containers, as well as musical instruments, pipes, and floats for fishing nets. By isolating the growing area for each, over the years seed growers have maintained the individual shapes and colorings of these ornamental gourds.

The varieties in the species cross easily; if all were grown together, many of the present forms would be altered and new forms would appear.

All types of gourds are fast growers if they have their quota of heat; warm nights are especially necessary.

Delay planting until the soil is warm. In short-season areas seed should be started indoors in pots 3 to 4 weeks earlier.

Set out transplants (or thin plants in the row) 2 feet apart.

About the edible Lagenaria. The seed companies offer two edible gourds (which, we believe, are really the same vegetable), belonging to the *Lagenaria siceraria* species.

Catalog (4) calls it "New Guinea Butter Vine" and says that the Italian edible gourd "will grow to enormous size—often 3-5 feet long and weighing 15 lbs. Similar to squash in growth, or can be trellised. Fruits should be eaten when small while the fuzz is still on them. Cook like squash or fry like eggplant."

Catalog (19) calls it *Lagenaria longissima* and describes it this way: "Italian vegetable used like summer squash if picked half-ripe. Has a rich full flavor. Delicious baked with fresh tomatoes, sprinkled with basil and olive oil. One customer from Boston wrote, 'They are so good, I eat them for breakfast.'"

Luffa aegyptiaca. Vegetable sponge, dishrag gourd. This fast-growing vine climbs to 10 to 15 feet, carrying cylindrical fruits 12 to 24 inches long.

Luffas are thought to come from tropical Asia, reaching China about 600 A.D. It is now cultivated throughout the tropics. Although it is a tropical gourd, the best luffas are grown in Japan.

To get the "sponge"—the fibrous interior—the ripe gourds are immersed in a tank of running water until the outer wall disintegrates. They then are bleached and dried in the sun.

Luffas are grown commercially for use as sponges and in the manufacture of many products—filters in marine and diesel engines, bath mats, table mats, sandals, and gloves.

In India the young tender fruits (not more than 4 inches long) are eaten

Gourds peeking out from under their leaf cover.

The Cultivated Members of the Gourd Family (Cucurbitaceae)

Genus	Species	Variety or common name
Cucurbita	pepo*	'Jack O'Lantern' pumpkin; 'Connecticut Field' pumpkin; 'Acorn' or 'Table Queen' squash; 'Vegetable Spaghetti,' 'Zucchini,' 'Yellow Crookneck,' and Bush Scallop summer squash; Small, hard-shell gourds; Edible gourd; Vegetable gourd
	moschata*	'Butternut squash;' 'Kentucky Field' pumpkin; 'Dickinson' pumpkin; 'Golden Cushaw' pumpkin
	maxima*	'Buttercup' squash; 'Hubbard' squash; 'Banana' squash; 'Sweetmeat' squash; 'Marblehead' squash; 'Turks' Turban' squash; 'Big Max' pumpkin; 'King of Mammoths' pumpkin
	ficifolia	Malabar gourd
	mixta*	'Green Striped Cushaw' pumpkin; 'White Cushaw' pumpkin
Lagenaria	siceraria	Bottle or White Flowered gourd; Cucuzzi
Luffa	cylindrica aegyptiaca	Dishrag gourd
Momordica	balsamina	Balsam apple
	charantia	Balsam pear
Sechium	edule	Chayote
Benincasa	hispida	Chinese Preserving melon or White Gourd of India
Cucumis	melo	Netted muskmelon or Cantaloupe ('Hales Best,' 'Harper Hybrid,' etc.); Honeydew & Casaba muskmelons (Honeydew, Crenshaw, etc.); Oriental Pickling melon; Dudaim melon; Snake or Serpent melon; Mango melon
	sativus	Cucumber, all varieties
	anguria	West Indian Gherkin
Citrullus	lanatus	Watermelon, all varieties; Citron
Trichosanthes	anguina	Snake or Serpent gourd

*See text about crossing between these species

'Green Striped Cushaw' pumpkin.

like cucumbers or cooked as a vegetable. According to *The Gourd* magazine, the small pods are used to replace edible podded peas in chop suey in Hawaii and China.

Luffa seeds are offered in the following seed catalogs: (19), (21), (26), (31).

'Turks Turban' squash. The catalogs offer this squash in both the decorative gourd section and in the winter squash varieties section.

'Vegetable Gourd'. This seems to be properly included in the *C. pepo* species, along with a mixture of squash and pumpkin. This is a vigorously growing vine whose foliage and fruits are attractive when trained on a trellis. The fruits are roundish, 3 to 5 inches across, and weigh about ½ pound. When mature, the gourd is striped a creamy white, mottled with dark green. The flesh is like a sweet winter squash. A favorite way to prepare this gourd is to stuff and bake it like bell peppers, with meat and rice.

Except for perhaps the mustard family, the gourd family has the greatest diversity in its edible forms, and certainly the widest variation in color and form of fruit among the vegetables. If you cross two varieties of summer squash, such as zucchini or yellow crookneck, with white bush scallop, the second generation will produce an unbelievable array of colors, shapes, textures, and sizes of fruit. You can grow hundreds, and no two will be alike.

The pumpkin and squash seeds that you buy come from seeds of the variety that's grown in isolated plots, free from the pollen of any other variety. However, nature has a way of sneaking in a cross or two. These will show up as occasional strange plants when you plant commercial seed in your garden. If you save seeds from the odd ones, you will get many different forms the next year.

Possibilities for crossing. These can be summarized as follows: Any two or more varieties *of the same species* will cross freely. For example, 'Hubbard' and 'Buttercup' squash will cross, as will 'Harper Hybrid', 'Hales Best', and 'Crenshaw' melons.

The only crossing that occurs *between species* is in the genus *Cucurbita*. *C. pepo* will cross with *C. moschata*. *C. maxima* will cross with *C. moschata*. However, *C. pepo* will not cross with *C. maxima*. An additional cross, *C. pepo* with *C. mixta*, also will occur. Therefore we know that 'Acorn' squash will cross with 'Butternut' squash, but 'Acorn' will not cross with 'Hubbard' squash.

Other crosses between species, such as muskmelon with cucumber *(Cucumis melo* x *C. sativus)* do not occur, nor do any crosses occur between one genus and another.

Horseradish

This old plant has survived through the centuries. It's a native of Eastern Europe from the Caspian through Russia and Poland to Finland. Planted in colonial American gardens, horseradish spread to flourish as a wild plant.

Since horseradish rarely produces seed, it generally is grown from root cuttings. Set the cuttings small end down, and place the large end 2 to 3 inches below the soil surface. Plant 12 inches apart. The roots you set out in spring will be the right size for harvesting in the fall.

Some growers set the cuttings on a slant rather than vertically. When the leaves are about a foot high, the root becomes partially exposed; do not remove the small branched roots at the base. Re-cover the roots to get a quality root. Repeat this operation about a month later.

Since horseradish makes its greatest growth in late summer and early fall, don't harvest it until October or November. Catalog sources include: (4), (5), (10), (12), (15), (21).

Serving ideas. Beloved for its hot taste, this root plays a role in cuisines throughout the world.

Peel and grate the root and blend with heavy whipped cream or sour cream to accompany sauerbrauten or roast pork.

Serve freshly grated horseradish as a side dish to *pot-au-feu.*

Add the grated root to a white sauce to accompany roast beef or tongue.

Husk tomato, or tomatilla.

Husk Tomato

Also called ground cherry, poha berry, and strawberry tomato, this tomato relative is grown like tomatoes and is about the same size as the cherry tomato. The ornamental Chinese Lantern plant is a close relative. The fruits of the husk tomato are produced inside a paperlike husk. When ripe, the husks turn brown and the fruits drop from the plant. If left in the husks they will keep for several weeks. The fruit is sweeter than the small-fruited tomatoes and is used in pies and jams, or it may be dried in sugar and used like raisins. Hawaii's *poha* jam is husk tomato jam.

Burgess Seed & Plant Company offers this recipe for ground cherry preserves:

Remove the husks from ground cherries. Make a syrup of 1½ cups sugar, 3 cups water, and juice of 2 lemons. Boil 5 minutes. Add enough cherries to reach the top of the syrup. Boil slowly until the cherries are tender and clear. If desired, can and seal in sterilized jars, as you would other fruit.

In place of the lemon, you could add 1/3 as many sliced tart apples, then cook until both apples and ground cherries are thick and clear.

Tomatilla or jamberry. Very similar to the husk tomato in growth habit but the fruit is larger and fills the husk completely.

Jerusalem Artichoke

This vegetable entered colonial American gardens under a very misleading common name and has suffered that handicap ever since. It is in no way related to the artichoke, nor does the Jerusalem in the name have any connection with the Holy Land.

The Jerusalem artichoke comes from eastern North America. In 1616, early explorers found the Indians using it, and carried it back to the Old World under the Italian name *Girasole,* which means "turning to the sun." It is thought that some mumbling of that name turned it into "Jerusalem" to non-Italian ears.

European botanists classified it as *Helianthus tuberosus,* or a tuberous sunflower.

It's a perennial, growing 6 to 10 feet high, with the look of a rough sunflower.

How to grow. Start with tubers, the same way as you would potatoes.

The harvest begins about 100 to 105 days after planting. Jerusalem artichokes can be left in the ground over winter.

Serving ideas. You can prepare the Jerusalem artichokes in all ways that you would potatoes—but with an important difference: the Jerusalem artichoke is delicious raw and never should be overcooked. Use raw slices as a last-minute garnish in clear soups. Use lightly boiled tubers in salads with oil and vinegar dressing. Slowly sauté quartered tubers in butter, just until they are tender.

Kale

Kale and collards are closely related to cabbage. They have been cultivated for as long as any vegetable has been grown. Although they are similar in many ways, collards and kale differ in one respect: collards produce through hot summers; kale can't take the heat. Both are extremely hardy.

How to grow. Kale grows best in the cool days of fall. Frost even improves the flavor of the leaves. Since kale thinnings make good eating, scatter the seeds in a 4-inch band, and thin finally to 8 to 12 inches in rows 18 to 24 inches apart.

For early planting in the spring, use transplants; but for fall planting, direct seeding is best.

Time to sow seeds in place (for dates, see Cabbage, page 82).

Varieties. These varieties of edible kale also deserve a place in the flower border: 'Blue Curled Scotch' (55 days to maturity). Leaves, as curled as parsley, are a distinct blue-green.

'Dwarf Siberian Curled' (65 days). The grayish-green leaves are held upright like plumes.

Both grow to 12 to 18 inches tall, and as wide.

Kohlrabi

Kohlrabi, a relatively recent development from wild cabbage, comes from northern Europe. It was not known until about 500 years ago, and was first recorded in the United States as recently as about 1800.

This unusual but little-known vegetable deserves to be grown and appreciated more. It looks like a turnip growing on top of the ground, sprouting leaves all over.

In fact, it often is described as a turnip growing on cabbage roots. The flavor is reminiscent of both turnip and cabbage, but it is milder and sweeter than either.

How to grow. Grow in the same way as turnips (see page 138). Woody stem fibers develop through the edible portion when kohlrabi is fully developed—usually when they are about 2 to 3 inches in diameter.

Time to sow seeds in place (for dates, see Beets, page 80).

Varieties. The two varieties commonly grown are: 'Early White Vienna' and 'Early Purple Vienna'.

'Early White Vienna' (55 days). Light green color, most commonly grown.
'Early Purple Vienna' (60 days). Light purple.

Both these forms are attractive and unusual enough to be included in the ornamental vegetable border. A new variety is 'Grand Duke' (45 days), with a crisp, sweet bulb and designated as an All-America Selection.

Serving ideas. Prepare kohlrabi as you would turnips. It is excellent on a *Bagna*

Kale—a member of the large cabbage family.

Cauda tray (see page 141), or as a vegetable relish with sour cream dips. Cube and add it to stews, or mash it with butter and cream.

Kohlrabi—another member of the cabbage family.

Leeks

Leeks take a good 80 days to grow from transplants; 140 days to grow from seed. If you grow the leeks from seed, sow the seed in late winter and thin to about 3 inches between plants.

Unlike onions, leeks do not bulb. Hill soil around the thickened stems to blanch them. To get long white stems, plant the leeks in trenches 4 to 6 inches deep, and when the plants are fairly well grown, hill soil against the stems. The most popular variety is 'Large American Flag'.

Serving ideas. To remove the sandy grit that burrows deep inside the stalks, wash the stalks thoroughly by trimming the ends and slicing them lengthwise, then holding them under running water. Use leeks in quiches, stews, and soups.

Immature leeks—a necessary vegetable in the gourmet's kitchen.

Lettuce

Leaf lettuce, native to the Mediterranean and Near East, goes back to antiquity. More than 2500 years ago, it was cultivated in the royal gardens of the Persian kings.

Growing lettuce successfully means not only growing a quality crop but also bringing it in for many months of the year, in quantities that can always be used.

If you can plan for harvesting a salad combining wedges of tomatoes, slices of green peppers and cucumbers, and 3 kinds of lettuce, you can consider yourself a true vegetable grower.

Varieties

Crisphead. Also known as iceberg. If there is only one lettuce in the produce display, this will be it.

1. Romaine and 'Salad Bowl' lettuce.
2. Cos or Romaine lettuce.
3. A 'Bibb' variety.

'Great Lakes' (82 to 90 days to maturity). Slow to bolt. Crisp, serrated leaves. May be bitter in hot weather.

'Ithaca' (72 days). Mild, nonbolting, and tipburn-resistant in all seasons. May break down in late fall weather.

'Imperial 44', and '456' (84 days). Heads are medium to small. Adapted to spring and summer growing

'Pennlake' (70 days). Best in spring. Large and tender.

'Oswego' (70 days). 'Fulton' (80 days). Similar to 'Ithaca'.

Most frequently recommended for the West: 'Pennlake' in spring, 'Ithaca' in spring and summer, and 'Great Lakes' for the fall crop or winter crop in mild-winter areas.

Most frequently recommended varieties for the South are: 'Great Lakes', 'Imperial 456' and '847', and 'Pennlake'. Great Lakes strains hold up well in fall plantings.

Most frequently recommended varieties for the North and Northeast: 'Great Lakes', 'Fulton', 'Ithaca', and 'Pennlake'.

Butterhead. A heading type, in which the leaves are loosely folded. Outer leaves may be green or brownish. Inner leaves are cream or butter colored. Butterhead types are not favored commercially because they bruise and tear easily, but this is no problem in the home garden.

'Big Boston' (75 days). Medium size. Leaves are broad, smooth, thick, and crisp. Bolts easily. Needs cool weather.

'Dark Green Boston' (73 to 80 days). Loosely folded. Thick, substantial leaves.

'Deer Tongue' or 'Matchless' (80 days). Thick green leaves with succulent midribs. Tightly folded.

'Bibb' (75 days). A small head, 3½ inches across. The small, dark green leaves are folded loosely. Bolts in warm weather.

'Summer Bibb' (77 days). Has the quality of 'Bibb', but is slow to bolt.

'Buttercrunch' (75 days). Thick leaves, more vigorous than 'Bibb'. Heat resistant and slow to bolt.

'Butter King' (70 days). Large and vigorous. Slow bolting.

'Tom Thumb' (65 days). A miniature butterhead type.

Most frequently recommended varieties for the West are: 'Buttercrunch', 'Summer Bibb', and 'Dark Green Boston'.

Most frequently recommended varieties for the South are: 'Bibb', 'Summer Bibb', and 'Buttercrunch'.

Recommended varieties for the North and Northeast are: 'Buttercrunch', 'Summer Bibb', and 'Dark Green Boston'.

Leaf lettuce or bunching. More or less open in growth. There are many variations in outer leaves; some are frilled and crumpled, some are deeply lobed. The leaf color varies from light green to red and brownish red.

'Black Seeded Simpson' (44 days). Light green, moderately crinkled leaves.

'Prizehead' or 'Bronze Leaf' (45 days). Large, broad bronze-tinted leaves. Mild in flavor. Vigorous.

'Salad Bowl' (40 days). Crinkly leaves in a broad clump. Tender. Heat resistant and slow to bolt.

'Oakleaf' (40 days). Medium size. Withstands heat.

'Grand Rapids' (45 days). Frilled and crinkled.

'Slobolt' (45 days). The 'Grand Rapids' type stands more heat.

'Ruby' (50 days). Give it high marks for color.

The varieties most frequently recommended are:

'Salad Bowl', 'Prizehead', 'Black Seeded Simpson' and 'Grand Rapids'.

Cos or romaine. Grows upright 8 to 9 inches tall, with tightly folded leaves. Medium green outer leaves and greenish white interior.

'Dark Green Cos' and 'Paris Island Cos' are widely adapted and available.

'Ruby' and 'Butter' lettuce.

Time to sow seeds in place (sow seeds indoors 3-5 weeks earlier)

Zone/South		Zone/North		Zone/West	
1	1/1-1/30, 9/1-12/31	**5**	3/1-4/20, 8/10-9/15	**6, 8, 13**	4/1-7/15
2	1/1-2/15, 9/15-12/31	**6**	3/20-4/30, 8/1-8/30	**9**	5/15-7/1
3	1/15-3/15, 9/1-10/10	**7**	4/1-5/15, 7/15-8/15	**10**	6/10-7/30
4	2/1-3/15, 9/1-10/10	**8**	4/15-5/30, 7/1-7/30	**12**	5/1-7/31
5	2/15-3/31, 8/1-9/15	**9**	5/15-7/1	**14**	9/1-12/31
6	3/1-4/15, 8/15-9/15	**10**	6/10-7/30	**15, 21**	1/1-2/28, 8/1-8/31,
7	4/1-5/15, 7/15-8/15	**11**	4/25-5/1		11/1-12/31
13	4/1-7/15			**16, 17**	4/1-8/15
				18	1/1-11/30
				19	1/1-8/30, 11/1-12/31
				20	2/1-8/30
				22	1/1-2/28, 8/1-8/31, 11/1-12/31

Lettuce is a cool-season vegetable. The longer days and warmer nights of summer encourage flowering—"bolting to seed." By carefully choosing slow-bolting varieties, you may bring some lettuce through the summer. Extend the harvest by making a succession of small plantings. If sunlight in your garden is clear-sky intense, plant the summer lettuce in partial shade. A little protection will stretch harvests months beyond the normal season. See page 55.

How to grow. For head lettuce, sow seed ¼ to ½ inch deep. Thin to 12 to 14 inches between plants in rows 18 to 24 inches apart. You can transplant thinnings for a somewhat later harvest, buy transplants at your garden center, or grow your own indoors. For summer lettuce, try germinating your own transplants indoors where it is cooler than the garden. Lettuce requires cool conditions for germination.

For leaf lettuce, sow seed ¼ to ½ inch deep. Thin to 4 to 6 inches between plants in the first thinning, and to 6 to 10 on the final thinning, depending on the size of the variety.

Fertilizing and watering. Even though lettuce occupies the soil for a relatively short time, every day must be a growing day. Provide an adequate supply of nutrients and moisture.

Fertilize the soil before you plant by adding 3 to 4 pounds of 5-10-10 per 100 square feet. (See page 40.) If a young plant's growth is checked by lack of nutrients, it never fully recovers.

Never let the plant suffer from lack of moisture. It needs water most critically when the heads begin to develop.

Mistakes beginners make. Although you may find it difficult to thin any vegetable ruthlessly, lettuce offers a good rationalization: you can eat the leaves you pull off. In fact, thinning is a real necessity. If you leave 2 plants of head lettuce in the space where only 1 should grow, you get 2 poor heads.

You can harvest some open-leaf lettuce varieties a leaf at a time, but with most varieties the best part is the tender, light green material in the center of the almost-mature plant. If you leave the row crowded with plants, you get a bunch of little, bitter, outside leaves.

Melons

You can't grow all the melon types in every home garden, but considering the new, early maturing varieties of crenshaw and honeydew, and early varieties of cantaloupes, the choice is wider than you might think.

How to grow. To grow melons successfully:

1. Give preference to disease-resistant varieties whenever possible.
2. Start seed indoors in containers. (See page 53.)
3. When the weather warms, set out transplants in a black plastic film mulch. (See page 50.)
4. Cover young plants with hot caps or clear plastic film. With the exception of the newer bush varieties most melons need space to grow, so space them 12 inches apart in rows 4 to 6 feet apart.

Fertilizing-watering. Before planting, work 5-10-10 into the soil at the rate of 4 pounds per 100 feet of row. Make a second application of the same amount when the runners are 12 to 18 inches, spreading the fertilizer 8 inches away from the plants. Make the third application after the first melons are set. Vines require plenty of moisture while they're growing and up to the time they are fully grown. But hold back on watering during the ripening period.

Harvesting melons (muskmelons, cantaloupes). "Full slip" is the guide for ripeness of melons that are shipped to market. It means that the stem breaks away cleanly with slight pressure. That's not the same as "vine ripe," however. For this, wait until the stem breaks away when you just lift the melon.

Time to sow seeds in place (can be started indoors 3-4 weeks earlier)

Zone/South	Zone/North	Zone/West	
1 2/1-3/10	**5** 5/15-6/15	**6, 8, 13** —	
2 2/15-3/30	**6** 5/1-6/30	**9** 6/1-6/10	
3 3/1-4/10	**7** 5/10-6/20	**10** —	
4 3/15-4/30	**8** 5/20-6/10	**12** 5/15-6/30	
5 4/1-4/30	**9** 6/1-6/10	**14** —	
6 4/15-6/15	**10** —	**15, 21** 3/1-4/30	
7 5/15-6/15	**11** 5/20-6/15	**16, 17** 5/1-6/15	
13 —		**18** 4/1-4/30	
		19 3/1-4/30	
		20 2/1-4/30	
		22 1/1-4/30, 7/1-7/31	

Varieties. The varieties most frequently recommended in the northern and western growing regions are (disease resistance is indicated [PM] Powdery Mildew, [F] Fusarium Wilt):

'Burpee Hybrid' (85 days to maturity). Good, medium-musky flavor. 3¾-pound fruit. Small seed cavity. Outstanding in all trials.

'Harper's Hybrid' (86 days) (F). Mild flavor with high sugar content. Thick-fleshed, 3½-pound fruit. Small cavity.

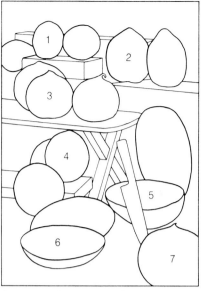

A melon family portrait: **1.** Muskmelon. **2.** Crenshaw. **3.** Casaba. **4.** Honey Dew. **5.** Watermelon. **6.** Christmas melon. **7.** Casaba.

'Gold Star' (87 days) (F). Bright orange color, strong musky flavor, 3-pound fruit.

'Saticoy Hybrid' (90 days) (F) (PM). Medium-musky flavor. 3½-pound, thick-fleshed fruit.

You can grow the early varieties of crenshaw and honeydew wherever the above varieties are successful.

'Early Crenshaw' (90 days). Thick, salmon-pink flesh. Oval fruits to 14 pounds. Dark green skin turns yellowish-green when ripe.

'Honey Mist' (92 days). High sugar. Greenish-white flesh. Compares with the finest honeydews. Seed sources: (5), (19). A number of extra-early varieties of muskmelons adapted to short-season areas—for example, the midget variety 'Minnesota Midget'—are listed in the catalogs. Matures in 60 days. Produces 4-inch melons on 3-foot vines; from the University of Minnesota.

'Hales Best Jumbo' (82 days to maturity). 3- to 4-pound fruits. Thick, deep salmon flesh.

'Gulfstream' (85 days) (DM) (PM). 2 to 3 pounds. Mild flavor.

'Planter Jumbo' (86 days) (DM) (PM). 4 pounds. Vigorous vines. Deep orange flesh.

'Edisto 47' (88 days) (DM) (PM). Alternaria resistant. firm sweet flesh, very small seed cavity. 5 pounds.

'Smith's Perfect' (90 days) (DM). Green rind turns tan when ripe. Aromatic flavor. 3½ pounds.

Coping with bitterness. "I planted cucumbers near the melons and they must have crossed. My melons taste like gourds." This complaint can be answered with all the backing of scientific research: "Cucumbers will not cross with melons." (See page 102.) But that won't satisfy you if you have bitter melons. Well, if the cucumbers didn't foul them up, what did?

Perhaps it's the way you watered them—or, more likely, a spell of cloudy, rainy weather as the fruits were ripening.

Mustard

There are many mustards. The species most frequently grown commercially is *Brassica juncea*, a native of the Orient. Several varieties, differing in shape and texture of leaf, are offered in seed packets, (see "Varieties"). Seed catalogs list another species, *B. campestris*, as mustard spinach or tendergreen mustard.

How to grow. Treat the same as lettuce. Sow seed in place in rows 12 to 18 inches apart, and thin to 4 to 8 inches apart as they become crowded. For tender leaves, give the plants plenty of fertilizer and water, and harvest them before they are full grown. Mustard grows quickly in fertile soil—25 to 40 days from seed to harvest.

When to plant. Mustard is a cool-weather, short-day crop and bolts to seed very early in the spring, or in August through September.

Varieties. 'Florida Broad Leaf' (about 50 days). Large, thick, green leaves with a whitish midrib.

'Southern Giant Curled' (about 40 days). Large, wide leaves grow upright; are bright green and yellow-tinged, with very curly edges.

'Fordhook Fancy' (about 40 days). Dark green leaves are deeply curled, fringed, and curved backward like an ostrich plume. Slow to bolt. Mild flavor.

'Tendergreen' or 'Spanish Mustard' (about 40 days). Good heat resistance. Produces a large rosette of thick, smooth, glossy, dark green leaves. One of the mildest in flavor.

Serving ideas. You can use these strong, distinctive greens instead of spinach in an Italian omelet or *frittata*, both of which are easy to prepare. As a vegetable dish, mustard greens taste best when cooked quickly in a small amount of boiling salted water. Dress them with olive oil and a splash of white wine vinegar, or finish them with a bacon and vinegar dressing.

Mustard

Nasturtium leaves and flowers

Nasturtium

This old-timer in the flower border and rock garden, used to cover fences and banks, grows quickly in full sun or part shade. Leaves are used in salads, like watercress. To get a plentiful supply of leaves, plant a trailing type in your landscape—or, if you haven't room for a trailer, plant a dwarf type in containers.

Okra-Gumbo

There are two types of okra: tall growers, which grow to 4 to 7 feet, and the so-called dwarf, which grows 2 to 4 feet tall. Its botanical name, *Hibiscus esculentus,* means that it is an edible hibiscus. You can plant it in the flower border as an annual hibiscus and enjoy its hollyhocklike flowers.

A half dozen plants will give you more than enough over a long season for the cupful you'll need now and then for chicken gumbo, stews, and soups.

Okra is a warm-season vegetable. Follow the planting dates and the fertilizing and watering schedule for corn.

Give it space to grow—36 to 48 inches between rows. Thin to 8 to 10 inches apart in the row.

In short-season areas, start seeds in small pots about 5 weeks before you would plant corn or beans. Set the seedlings out when the soil is thoroughly warm.

Varieties. 'Clemson Spineless' grows to 4 to 5 feet tall and is a heavy yielder. 'Perkins Spineless' is a dwarf that grows to 2½ to 3 feet.

Special handling. To keep the plant producing, let no pod ripen on the stalk. Young pods are more tender and more nutritious.

Okra

Onions

The onion has been highly regarded since antiquity. Onions fed the sweating pyramid-builders and the conquering troops of Alexander the Great. General Grant wrote a dispatch to the war department, saying: "I will not move my armies without onions."

Emperor Nero earned the nickname "leek-throated" because he often munched on leeks to "clear his throat."

An enthusiastic 19th-century gourmet said it all for onion lovers everywhere: "Without onions there would be no gastronomic art. Banish it from the kitchen and all pleasure of eating flies with it . . . its absence reduces the rarest dainty to insipidity, and the diner to despair."

The familiar dry onion is a weather-wise plant.

The onion naturally grows tops in cool weather and forms bulbs in warm weather. But both temperatures and day length control the timing of the bulbing. Varieties are classed as long-day and short-day.

In the North, most varieties require 14 to 16 hours of daylight. In the South, onion varieties designed to grow through the cool fall and winter months are triggered to bulb at about 12 hours, as the weather warms in early summer.

'Yellow Bermuda' and 'Excel' are standard short-day varieties. Because of early bulbing, they make a small bulb in the North. However, if you plant good-sized transplants early, you will get a larger bulb. To get the very small "Pearl" or pickling onions in the North, thickly plant the short-day variety 'Eclipse' in late April to May. This variety develops normal-sized bulbs when grown in winter in the South.

Onions are heavy feeders, so work manure and fertilizer into the soil before planting. A pound of manure to each square foot of ground and 4 to 5 pounds of 5-10-10 fertilizer per 100 square feet will do the job.

Onions need a constant supply of moisture, especially during the bulb-enlargement stage. New growth stops from the center when bulbing starts.

How to grow. Start from seeds, transplants, or sets. Onions are easiest to grow from sets, but the varieties available as sets are limited. You can get seedlings at garden centers and through mail-order seed companies.

A young plant at the "green onion" stage.

If you start from seed, sow them ½ inch deep, and thin them to 2 to 3 inches, in rows 12 to 24 inches apart.

The onion family includes scallions, shallots, leeks, garlic, and chives—and countless varieties of yellow, red, and white onions.

Harvesting. When the bulbs are ripe, the tops begin to yellow and fall over. When about ¾ of them have fallen, use a rake to break over those still standing. When all the tops are dead, pull up the plants and spread them in the sun for 3 or 4 days. Place the tops over the bulbs. Then cut the tops off about an inch from the bulb. Store onions in mesh bags in a cool dry location.

Time to sow seeds in place (can be started indoors 8 weeks earlier)

Zone/South	Zone/North	Zone/West
1 1/1-3/31, 9/10-11/15	**5** 3/1-4/15	**6, 8, 13** 4/1-5/15
2 1/1-3/31, 9/1-10/31	**6** 3/10-4/30	**9** 4/15-5/31
3 1/1-2/28, 8/15-9/30	**7** 4/1-5/15	**10** 5/1-5/31
4 1/15-3/15, 8/10-9/15	**8** 4/10-5/31	**12** 4/1-5/5
5 2/1-3/15, 8/1-8/31	**9** 4/15-5/31	**14** 3/10-5/15
6 3/1-4/15	**10** 5/1-5/31	**15, 21** 1/1-2/28, 11/1-12/31
7 4/1-5/15	**11** 4/25-5/20	**16, 17** 2/15-4/30
13 4/1-5/15		**18** 1/1-3/31
		19 1/1-3/31
		20 1/1-2/28, 11/1-12/31
		22 1/1-1/30, 11/1-12/31

Varieties. 'Yellow Sweet Spanish' (Utah). Large yellow bulb. Mild sweet flesh. Medium keeper. Good slicer. Thrips resistant. Rec: All zones.

'White Sweet Spanish' (Utah). Largest white. Firm. Mild sweet flesh. Medium keeper. Plants generally are available. North; West.

'Early Yellow Globe'. Medium-sized globe. Firm flesh. Pungent taste. Good keeper. North; West.

'Southport Yellow Globe'. Medium-sized globe. Firm and pungent. All zones.

'Yellow Globe Danvers'. Medium sized. Flattened globe. Firm and pungent. Plants generally are available. All zones.

'Yellow Bermuda'. Flat blub. Soft mild flesh. Short keeper. Southwest; South.

'Early Grano'. Straw-colored. Top-shaped bulb. Soft mild flesh. Short keeper. West.

'California Early Red'. Medium-red color. Flattened globe. Soft mild flesh. Short keeper. West.

'Excel'. Flat bulb shape. Yellow, firm, sweet, mild flesh. Resistant to pink root. Good keeper. Fall planting. South.

'Crystal White Wax'. Soft, mild, white flesh. Short storage. For fall planting. South.

'Southport White Globe'. Medium-sized globes. Firm and pungent. Good keeper. Plant in spring. South.

'Ebenezer' (105 days). Large bulb. Firm flesh. Pungent. North.

Parsnips

This Mediterranean native goes back to antiquity. The Romans collected wild parsnips from fields. The 1st-century Emperor Tiberius imported them from Germany.

By the 16th century, parsnips were common in Europe. The early colonists brought them to North America, where the Indians enjoyed their sweet nutty flavor and grew them in their gardens.

How to grow. Since the roots develop to a length of 12 to 18 inches and become distorted in a heavy rough soil, parsnips grow best when grouped with carrots and salsify in deeply dug soil to which generous amounts of organic matter have been added, or in a raised bed. (One gardener's comment: "Hard digging is probably more of a problem than distortion. Extracting them from mud in winter is hard going.")

The seeds are slow to germinate—15 to 25 days. Sow 8, 12, or more seeds per foot, ½ inch deep, and cover the row with white plastic. (See page 51 about

Parsnips

plastic covering.) Remove the plastic when the seeds germinate. Later, thin them to 3 to 4 inches between plants in rows 16 to 24 inches apart.

The roots will take from 100 to 120 days to mature. To change the starch to sugar and give it the sweet nutlike flavor it's famous for, the roots must be subjected to winter cold near the freezing point.

Parsnip roots may be left in the ground all winter or dug out in the late fall and stored in moist sand. They can stand alternate freezing and thawing in the soil but are definitely damaged if frozen after harvest. U.S.D.A. Leaflet No. 545, *Growing Parsnips*, states: "There is no basis for the belief that parsnips that remain in the ground over the winter are poisonous. All reported cases of poisoning from eating so-called wild parsnips have been traced to Water Hemlock *(Cicuta)*, which belongs to the same family and resembles the parsnip somewhat. Avoid gathering wild plants that look like the parsnips."

Varieties. 'All American', 'Model', and 'Hollow Crown' are standard varieties.

Serving ideas. Parboil or steam parsnips in their skins, then peel and slice them lengthwise. If a large core has developed, cut it out. It's ready then to pan-glaze with butter and a touch of brown sugar and nutmeg for the best candied "sweet potatoes" you ever tasted. Or purée the boiled vegetables, blend in butter and cream, and top with buttered crumbs.

Peanuts

The Portuguese took this South American tropical plant from Brazil to West Africa. Spanish galleons carried peanuts from South America to the Philippines, and from there the plants spread to China, Japan, and India. Peanuts found a favorable climate in North America early in our history—Thomas Jefferson wrote about growing them in Virginia in 1781.

How to grow. There are two types—Virginia, with 2 seeds per pod, and Spanish, with 2 to 6 seeds per pod. Most of the Virginia forms are spreading; most of the Spanish are bunching. However, there are also bunching varieties of Virginia, that adapt better to short-season areas than the spreading types do.

Most varieties need a long, warm growing season of 110 to 120 days. If summers in your area are cool, however, forget peanuts as a crop, regardless of how long the season is. Catalog sources include: (4), (12), (15), (19), (25).

The strange growth habit of peanuts so intrigues gardeners that they will experiment with them, even when the plants must be grown in a container with special protection.

The plant resembles a yellow-flowering sweet pea bush. After the flowers wither, a stalklike structure known as a "peg" grows from the base of the flowers and turns down to penetrate the soil. When the peg pushes to a depth of 1 to 2½ inches, it moves into a horizontal position, at which point the pod begins to form.

The soil should be light and sandy. Peanuts require a generous supply of calcium in the top 3 or 4 inches of soil, where the pods develop. To help in this regard, you can dust the foliage with gypsum at the time of flowering.

Sow seeds (shelled) 1½ inches deep, 2 or 3 to the foot. Thin to 6 to 10 inches apart in rows 30 inches apart. Make sure the plants get a regular supply of water up to 2 weeks before harvest. You'll need to cultivate shallowly to prevent damage to peanuts near the top of the soil.

When the plants are about 12 inches tall, mound soil around the base of the plants and cover with a mulch.

When the plants turn yellow at the end of the season, pull up the whole plant. You should find a flock of peanuts hanging by their pegs.

Before stripping the peanuts from the plants, let them cure in a warm airy place for 2 to 3 weeks.

To roast peanuts without scorching them, place the unshelled nuts in a colander or wire basket. Preheat the oven to 500°. Place the peanuts in the oven. Turn the oven off. When the peanuts are cool to the touch, they're ready to eat.

Green peas in a pod.

Peas

Southerners call these "English peas," to distinguish them from cowpeas.

English peas are a cool-season crop. They are grown in early spring to midsummer in the cooler sections, but in fall, winter, and very early spring in the warmer areas.

How to grow. The low-growing varieties that don't require staking are the easiest to handle. Plant these in rows 18 to 24 inches apart. The tall growers trained on chicken wire or trellis need 36 inches between rows, but you can plant them in double rows 6 inches apart on either side of the trellis.

Time to sow seeds in place

Zone/South		Zone/North		Zone/West	
1	1/1-2/28. 11/1-12/31	**5**	3/5-4/10	**6, 8, 13**	3/5-5/31
2	1/1-3/31. 12/1-12/31	**6**	3/15-4/30	**9**	4/15-5/15
3	1/15-3/15. 8/15-9/15	**7**	3/20-5/20	**10**	4/20-5/31
4	2/1-3/31. 8/1-8/31	**8**	4/1-5/20	**12**	3/15-6/15
5	2/15-4/10. 7/20-8/15	**9**	4/15-5/15	**14**	1/1-2/28. 8/1-10/30
6	3/10-4/15. 7/5-8/10	**10**	4/20-5/31	**15, 21**	9/1-12/31
7	3/20-5/20	**11**	4/25-5/1	**16, 17**	2/10-6/15. 7/20-8/5
13	3/5-5/31			**18**	1/1-7/31
				19	1/1-3/31. 8/1-8/31. 12/1-12/31
				20	1/1-7/31
				22	1/1-1/30. 11/1-12/31

Varieties. 'Alaska' (55 to 60 days). Its earliness is its chief virtue. This bush type grows 24 to 28-inch vines. These small peas are lower in sugar than others listed here. Good for canning.

'Green Arrow' (70 days). A heavy producer of sweet peas in 4-inch pods.

'Sugar Snap' (70 days) is an exceptional variety, which can be eaten pod and all. Sweet and delicious, raw or cooked. Well-filled with peas. All-America Selection.

'Little Marvel' (63 days) and 'Progress No. 9' (62 days). Good producers of top-quality peas on 18-inch vines.

'Wando' (64 days). A sturdy short grower, is more heat tolerant.

Snow Peas or Sugar Peas, see Edible Podded Sugar Peas

Peppers

In his search for a new route to the spice-laden Indies, Columbus had a different pepper in mind than what he found in the New World. The black and white pepper of the salt-and-pepper set comes from the berries and seeds of *Piper nigrum*, which is in no way related to the peppers of the genus *Capsicum* that Columbus found growing in Indian gardens in the Caribbean. When he returned to Spain, he described his find as "pepper more pungent than that of the Caucasus." Spice-hungry Europeans immediately adopted the new vegetable. Within 50 years, peppers grew in England; in less than a century, they grew on Austrian crown lands. In India, they became so common that some botanists thought them indigenous.

Peppers are classed as a hot-weather vegetable, but their requirements are not as high as generally supposed. The fruit set occurs in a rather limited range of night temperatures. The blossoms drop when night temperatures fall much below 60° or rise above 75°. Peppers thrive in areas with daytime temperatures around 75° and night temperatures of 62°. A high daytime temperature —above 90°— will cause blossoms to drop excessively. However, fruit setting will resume when normal weather resumes. The small-fruited varieties are more tolerant of high temperatures than the large ones.

Peppers seem to have a self-regulating mechanism that keeps them from overloading the plant. When the plant already has a full quota of fruit underway, all new blossoms drop. When some of the peppers are harvested, the plant again will set fruit—if the weather is right.

How to grow. The easiest way to start is to buy transplants at your garden store. You can generally find the varieties of sweet peppers adapted to your area. Growing your own transplants from seed is not difficult (see "Planting and Care," page 48).

Don't set out transplants until the weather definitely has warmed. Each year many gardeners must learn the same lesson over again: if the night temperatures fall below 55°, your small plants will just sit, turn yellow and become stunted. So try to resist the temptation to put these and other warm-weather vegetables out in the garden too soon.

Some gardeners deliberately set out more plants than they need and then, after a few weeks of growth, pull out the weaklings. If you do this, give the plants space to grow: set them 24 inches apart, in rows 30 to 36 inches apart.

When the first blossoms open, give the plants a light application of fertilizer. Water it in well—any stress from lack of moisture at flowering time may cause blossom drop. Add a mulch to conserve moisture and stop weeds.

When it's time to pick the peppers, use pruning shears or a sharp knife.

Decorative in containers. Peppers have many esthetic qualities that make them ideal as container plants (in tubs, boxes, or large pots) for patio, porch, or terrace, or as ornamentals in the flower border. They have shiny green leaves, small white flowers, and fruits in many shapes and colors—green, yellow, and red. The small bushy peppers and the herb basil are good companion plants, destined for the same stove top sauce pan.

Time to set out plants (sow seeds indoors 7-9 weeks earlier)

Zone/South	Zone/North	Zone/West
1 1/1-2/28, 8/1-10/31	**5** 4/20-6/15	**6, 8, 13** 5/15-6/15
2 2/1-3/31	**6** 5/1-6/30	**9** 5/25-6/30
3 3/1-4/30	**7** 5/15-6/30	**10** 6/1-6/30
4 4/1-5/31	**8** 5/20-6/30	**12** 3/1-4/30
5 4/15-5/31	**9** 5/25-6/30	**14** 5/1-7/5
6 4/20-6/10	**10** 6/1-6/30	**15, 21** 4/1-5/31
7 5/15-6/30	**11** 6/1-6/15	**16, 17** 5/1-7/5
13 5/15-6/15		**18** 5/1-5/31
		19 3/1-5/31
		20 4/1-7/10
		22 5/1-5/31

The shorter the growing season, the more reason to choose the "extra early" varieties. Adaptation varies by area.

Varieties. Some of the hot varieties that are especially attractive in containers:

'Hungarian Wax'. An early, hot, pickling variety about 5 inches long. Slender, with a blunt end. The plant grows 12 to 15 inches high and is very prolific under favorable conditions. The fruit is a clear yellow, maturing to bright red.

'Red Chili'. A well-behaved plant growing to 18 inches tall, it carries its 2-inch-long, tapered fruits upright on its branches. Both of these peppers are really hot. They are used extensively for pepper sauces.

'Dutch Treat' (70 days). Clusters of yellow peppers. All-America Selection.

'Fresno Chili'. Similar in growth habit to 'Red Chili', but somewhat taller. The fruits are 3 inches long and taper to a point. A prolific bearer of very hot peppers.

1. 'California Wonder'
2. 'Burpee Fordhook'
3. 'Sweet Banana'

'Long Red Cayenne'. Grows vigorously to 24 to 30 inches tall. The fruits are 4 to 5 inches long and conical or finger-shaped. It is adapted to a wide growing range and is an early maturing variety. The peppers are used to make pickles and for drying.

The big bells. These large, blocky sweet peppers are shaped ideally for stuffing. Most often they are used when green, but they will turn red (becoming sweeter and mellower) if grown for a longer period. Some varieties in this group are 'Bell Boy', 'Keystone Resistant Giant', 'Pennwonder', and 'Yolo Wonder'. All mature in about 75 to 80 days. 'Early Calwonder' is ready for use in 65 to 70 days. The variety 'Golden Calwonder' turns a rich golden yellow at maturity.

Early season bells. There are a number of early varieties that bear smaller, less blocky peppers but produce them from 2 weeks to a month earlier than such standard bells as 'Yolo Wonder'.

'Early Bountiful'. Gives a high yield in a small space. Ripens red fruit a full month earlier than most large-fruited varieties.

'Vinette'. This dwarf plant grows about 14 inches tall. Will bear 8 to 10 moderately blocky but tapered fruits in 65 days. 'Vinedale' and 'Stokes Early Hybrid' are in this "early" class.

Peppers pictured above:
Hungarian Yellow Wax,
Serrano Chile, Sante Fe Grande,
Anaheim, Jalapeno,
Mercury Floral Gem

In a class by themselves. 'Anaheim Chili'. A vigorous, erect grower to 20 to 24 inches tall. The fruits are 6 to 8 inches long, tapering to a point. Medium hot. Boil them, skin them, and stuff them with cheese or meat, and you have *chili rellenos.*

'Sweet Banana'. The plant grows to 20 to 24 inches, with good foliage cover. The thick-walled fruits, 3½ to 4½ inches long, turn from yellow to red.

Drying peppers. You can dry both sweet and hot peppers for winter use. In Mexico, where all peppers are called "chiles," the dried peppers are ground daily in a mortar to make chili powder. A pinch of this powder will add flavor to almost any dish. You can vary the flavor by adding different amounts of powdered hot peppers.

Serving ideas. Hot peppers lend zing to many international dishes: Mexican salsas, Indian curries, African stews, and Spanish and Portuguese dishes.

In the U.S., we tend to use the large red and green sweet bell peppers more commonly. Cut them in strips and serve them raw on relish platters. Or serve in rings, strips, or diced in salads. Hollow them out and stuff them with lamb, beef, chicken, or shrimp mixtures and bake. Use in Chinese beef pepper steak or the French *ratatouille.*

Potato

The wild species of potatoes are grown from the southern United States all the way to southern Chile. The first cultivated varieties appeared in the Andes in South America, at altitudes above 6500 feet.

Spanish explorers brought the potato home with them, but the English, French, and Germans regarded it mainly as a curiosity for more than a century.

In America, potatoes became a fairly important crop after 1718, when many Presbyterians arrived from Ireland. Potatoes became a very significant crop right after 1846—the year of the devastating potato blight in Ireland.

Today, the potato exceeds all other crops in the world in volume and value. The largest producers are the Soviet Union and Germany.

New potatoes are easy to grow and provide a bountiful harvest from a small amount of space.

How to grow. Buy certified seed potatoes, or seed pieces, or "eyes" from garden stores or mail-order seed companies.

Good-sized seed pieces increase the chances for a good yield. Cut pieces about 1½ inches square. Be sure that each piece has at least one good eye.

The usual planting method is to set seed pieces, cut-side down, 4 inches deep and 12 inches apart in rows 24 to 36 inches apart. The tubers (the edible part) form on many stems rising from the seed piece. The potatoes do not grow in the roots, but form above the seed piece on underground stems.

When the plants are 5 to 6 inches high, scrape the soil from between the rows and hill up the plant, covering the stems with soil. If potatoes are exposed to light, either in the garden or storage, they turn green and become inedible.

Apply fertilizer in bands at both sides of the seed pieces when you plant. The best method is to make a 3-inch-deep and 6-inch-wide trench. Place the seed pieces in a row in the center, and work in fertilizer 1 to 2 inches deep at the edges of the trench.

Potatoes need a steady supply of moisture. If the soil dries out after the tubers begin to form, a second growth will start when the soil becomes moist, resulting in knobby potatoes or multiples.

Alternate wet and dry conditions will also cause "hollow heart," or cavities near the center of the tuber.

When to plant. Cool nights are needed for good tuber formation. (Gardeners who complain that their crop is "all tops and few potatoes" ignore the best planting dates in warm-summer areas.)

Mistakes beginners make. You can start potatoes from those you buy at the market. However, these may carry plant diseases and may have been treated to prevent sprouting. Freshly dug potatoes won't sprout until they have had a rest period. Other mistakes are overfertilizing before tubers are formed, ignoring the best planting dates, and permitting the tubers to turn green from exposure.

Special handling. Here is an old-time method of growing potatoes that you pick rather than dig: Set the seeds in a wide trench, 3 inches deep. As the stems grow, build up a covering of straw, pine needles, or any material that will protect them from the sun. (Cover the material with ½ inch of soil if wind is a problem.) The potatoes will form almost at ground level, and you can pick them up by pulling back the straw. You can pick early potatoes when the tops begin to flower. They will reach full size when the tops die down.

One potato vine will yield from 6 to 8 pounds of potatoes. We grew a few in the flower border and in boxes with good results.

Varieties for the northern and western growing regions: *Early.* 'Irish Cobbler', 'Norgold Russet', 'Norland', 'Red Pontiac', 'Superior', and 'White Rose'.
Late. 'Katahdin', 'Kennebec', and 'Russet Burbank—Netted Gem'.

Varieties for the South:
Early: 'Pontiac', 'Red LaSoda', 'Red Pontiac'. Late: 'Kennebec', 'Sebago'.

Pumpkin—see Squash

Radish

Give a youngster a package of radish seeds and say "go plant," and you'll have radishes. But to get crisp, mild, nonpithy radishes, you must provide the fundamentals of fertilizing and watering. Work fertilizers into the soil before planting so that they are available quickly to the young seedlings. Since spring radishes mature in 3 to 4 weeks from seeding, you don't have much time to correct your mistakes.

Thin seedlings 1 or 2 inches apart very soon after they emerge to reduce competition—roots begin to expand when they're only 2 weeks old. Scatter seeds spaced out in a 3- or 4-inch-wide row to reduce the need for thinning. For a continuous supply of crisp roots, start early with small plantings and repeat every 10 days.

Mistakes beginners make. The most frequent disaster among our panel gardeners was damage from the cabbage maggot. For how to control, see page 58.

Time to sow seeds in place (for dates, see Beets, page 80).

Varieties. For early and fall planting there are many shapes and sizes:
'Cherry Belle' (22 days to maturity). Round, cherry size, all red.
'Burpee White' (25 days). Round. Pick them when ¼ to 1 inch.
'French Breakfast' (24 days). Red with white tip, oblong.
'Sparkler' (25 days). Red with lower third white, round.
'White Icicle' (28 days). 5-inch-long roots.
'Champion' (28 days). Round, bright red. Pick from ½ to 1½ inches in diameter.

Winter varieties. Plant in late summer or fall to mature in fall or winter. These varieties become quite large but remain solid and nonbolting. If planted in spring and early summer, however, they may bolt.
'White Chinese' (50 days). Long, usually mild.
'China Rose' (52 days). Long, hot.
'Round Black Spanish' (56 days). Black, globe, hot.
Oriental fall and winter varieties: 'Takinashi' (65 days). 1 foot long, white, brittle fleshed. 'Sakurajima Mammoth' (70 days). Giant-sized to 70 pounds.

Serving ideas. Though traditionally considered a salad vegetable or relish, trimmed radishes are excellent butter-steamed until crisp-tender, about 5 minutes.

To get well-formed radishes, you must plant them where they can form quickly without interruption. Raised beds filled with a lightweight soil mix are ideal.

Be sure to thin radishes so that they have the room to form properly.

Salsify—Oyster Plant

The salsify root's flavor earned it the names, "vegetable oyster" and "oyster plant."

This plant will repay you for creating a deep crumbly soil by producing longer, straighter roots with fewer side roots.

Sow the seed ½ inch deep in rows 16 to 18 inches apart. When the seedlings are 2 inches high, thin them to 2 to 3 inches apart. Sow the seed as soon as the ground can be worked. The roots will be ready to harvest in the fall. You also can lift them and store them in damp sand to use through the winter, or leave them in the ground (if it is well drained). Salsify, like carrots and parsnips, does best in a raised bed filled with a special mix of organic matter and fine sand, vermiculite, or perlite.

The plant is usually a biennial, growing 2 to 3 feet high. It produces long-stemmed purplish flower heads the second year.

Scorzonera (black salsify). This is a relative of salsify. The long cylindrical roots have black skin but white flesh. You can leave the roots in the ground over winter; they will increase in size the second year. Black salsify bears dandelionlike yellow flowers on stems 2 to 3 feet high.

Serving ideas. Salsify and black salsify both are good raw with dips or cooked and masked with sauces such as hollandaise, mornay, and bechamel. To accompany fish, try these roots parboiled, then browned in butter. Their delicate flavor goes well with almost any meat.

Salsify.

Shallots

It is said that shallots were brought to Europe by French knights returning from the Crusades.

De Soto introduced them into the New World in 1532, in what is now Louisiana.

The shallot is a multiplier type of onion that divides into a clump of smaller, tuliplike bulbs. Most varieties set no seed. Catalog sources for shallots are (12), (19).

How to grow. Plant the cloves 1 inch deep, 2 to 4 inches apart with 12 to 18 inches between rows. Harvest when the tops die down in summer. Shallots are hardy and will overwinter as perennials, but for better results lift out the clusters of bulbs at the end of each growing season. Use the larger bulbs for cooking; replant the smaller ones in the fall.

Serving ideas. This sophisticated, delicate little onion lends superb flavor to a vinaigrette dressing for green salad and innumerable sauces. Stir finely chopped shallots into sour cream for a fast dressing for vegetables, meat loaves, and fish dishes.

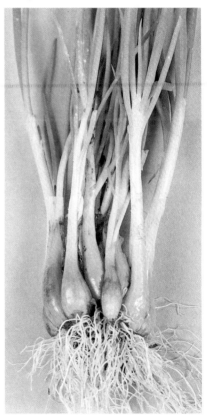

Shallots.

Soybeans

Soybeans were cultivated in China in 3000 B.C., and since earliest times they have been a basic food in Manchuria, Korea, and Japan. They first came to the United States in 1804, but they were used mainly as a forage crop until 1920. The big boom in commercial planting for seed began in 1942, as a result of the wartime demand for edible oils and fats. Today, soybeans are recognized as a superior home-garden vegetable. When using them as a fresh vegetable, pick the beans in the immature or green-shelled stage.

One characteristic that distinguishes the soybean from all other beans is its time clock. It gets its signal for flowering from the sky. Short nights (long days) delay flowering; long nights (short days) speed up flowering.

Most varieties have a narrow geographical range in which they will mature properly and produce a satisfactory crop.

The United States and Canadian researchers classify 9 maturity groups in the United States. Each has a narrow range of latitude, ranging from early varieties adapted to the short summers and long days of southern Canada and the northern states (group 0 to 1) to late-maturing varieties of the Gulf Coast (Group 8).

Varieties. The varieties available through mail-order seed companies are grouped as follows (the parenthetical numbers following each variety indicate the seed company that offers it—see page 140):

Group 0 and 1—'Disoy' (10); 'Early Hakucho' (19); 'Okuhara Early' (19); 'Giant Green' (44).

Group 2—'Verde' (21).

Group 3—'Kanrich' (4, 5, 11, 14, 19); 'Sodefuri' (19).

These groupings are based on full-season crops (crops planted in May that ripen in 120 to 130 days). When grown south of their adapted area, they mature earlier. In other words, all varieties listed will grow in the South and mature early. Check your seed catalog to be sure.

How to grow. Soybeans are as easy to grow as snap beans; treat them in the same way. Sow 6 to 8 seeds to the foot of the row, 1½ to 2 inches deep. Thin to 2 to 3 inches between plants in rows 24 to 30 inches apart.

You can plant early varieties as close as 2 feet. Later-maturing varieties require 3 feet.

Avoid cultivating or working around the beans when they are wet from rain, as the plants bruise and break easily.

Inoculation. Soybeans need to be inoculated with a commercial culture of nitrogen-fixing bacteria, unless you know that the bacteria already are in the soil. Soybean bacteria live in the soil for a number of years. Some farmers do not inoculate if a nodulated crop of soybeans has been grown on the field within the past 4 or 5 years. Others inoculate even though soybeans have been grown on the field recently.

Use inoculant prepared specifically for soybeans; inoculant containing bacteria from other legumes is not effective on soybeans. Follow the directions on the container.

In the absence of nodules, give nitrogen fertilizer for maximum yields.

When to harvest. Green beans are ready to use as soon as the pods are plump and the seeds are nearly full size but still green. All the beans on the plant ripen at about the same time, so you might as well pull the plant, find a shady spot, and settle down to pick the pods.

Serving ideas. Soybeans are not shelled like peas or lima beans. The best method is to pour boiling water over the pods and leave them in the hot water for 5 minutes, then drain and cool.

After this treatment it is easy to break the pods crosswise and squeeze out the beans.

Instead of shelling the beans first, try cooking the entire pod in salted boiling water. Then serve in the pod, squeezing out the seeds as you eat them. This is a common procedure in Japan, and it adds to the enjoyment—especially among the younger set.

Spinach

Spinach comes from Iran and adjacent areas. It had spread to China by 647 A.D., to Spain by 1100 A.D., and came to America with the first colonists in the 17th century.

How to grow. Spinach is a problem in the home garden. The plant has a short life before going to seed, and it is sensitive about temperatures.

Excellent substitutes for spinach are Swiss chard, New Zealand spinach, and Malabar spinach.

The big problem with spinach is its tendency to hurry on into its flowering

phase, which stops production of usable foliage. This change is controlled by day length, and it is highly related to variety. Long days hasten flowering; this effect is increased by low temperature early in the life of plants, and by high temperature in the later stage. All this makes bolting-susceptible varieties almost sure to fail if planted in spring. Therefore, use bolting-resistant (long-standing) varieties in spring. However, you can use some of the quick-bolting, otherwise-good varieties in the fall, and in winter in mild areas. In northern areas, make spring plantings as early as possible, and fall plantings about a month from the average frost date. In mild-winter areas, plant any time from about October 1 to March 1.

You also may need to consider varietal resistance to two important diseases: downy mildew (or blue mold), and spinach blight (or yellows). Varieties also differ as to whether they are savoyed (crinkled) or smooth. The savoy types are harder to clean, but they are thick, dark green, and usually preferred.

Varieties. *Long-standing varieties.* For spring planting, include:
  'Long Standing Bloomsdale' (48 days). Savoy, dark green.
  'America' (50 days). Savoy, dark green.
  'Winter Bloomsdale' (45 days). Smooth leaf, dark green, early.
  Other varieties. For fall and winter only, choose:
  'Virginia Savoy' (42 days). Savoy.
  'Hybrid No. 7' (42 days). Semisavoyed; resistance to downy mildew and blight.
  'Dixie Market' (40 days). Savoy, resistance to downy mildew.
  'Early Hybrid No. 8'. Semisavoy; resistance to downy mildew, blight.
  'Melody' (42 days). Widely adapted and good diseases resistance. All-America Selection.

Summer "spinach." In the summer months, when the cool-season spinach fails you, consider this trio of tropicals. These fresh "greens" compare well with true spinach in vitamins and flavor.

Malabar spinach (Basella alba). This attractive, glossy-leaved vine grows rapidly when the weather warms, producing edible shoots in 70 days. Train it against a fence or wall. You can cut young leaves and growing tips all summer. Use cooked or fresh in salads. Seed sources are (5), (25), and (31). See page 140.

New Zealand Spinach (Tetragonia expansa). This low-growing, ground-cover-type plant spreads to 3 or 4 feet across. You can cut the young tender stems and leaves repeatedly through the summer. The seeds, which really are bundles of seeds (like beet seeds), are slow to germinate. Start them indoors in peat pots and set them out after frost in spring. The seeds are widely available.

Tampala. This tropical is a cultivated variety of *Amaranthus tricolor*, and a close relative of the amaranthus of the flower garden. Those who grow it find it sweeter and more tasty than spinach. The tender young leaves need only a few minutes to cook. Catalog sources include: (4), (5).

Serving ideas. Cut the greens into 2- or 3-inch lengths and stir-fry with beef, garlic, and soy sauce for a fast Oriental dish.

Squash and Pumpkins

This group includes members of four species of the gourd family (see chart, page 103). All are native to the Americas. Most of our pumpkins and squashes originated in Mexico and Central America and were used all over North America by the American Indians. Most of our winter squashes originated in or near the Andes in northern Argentina.

How to grow. Since squashes and pumpkins (except for bush forms) use a lot of space, don't grow them if you're a mini-gardener unless you have vertical space available, such as a fence, a wall, a stout trellis, or even a compost pile. You can grow squashes and pumpkins with corn, but space them sparsely.

On the ground, the vining types need 10 feet or more between rows, but you can grow them in less space by training the vines or by pruning. You can cut off the long runners after some fruit are set, as long as a good supply of leaves remain to feed the developing fruit. Leave 2 to 4 feet between plants, depending on the vigor of the variety. Bush types do best in rows 5 or 6 feet apart, but the plants can be as close as 16 to 24 inches apart.

Direct seeding is best, but in short-season areas, you can gain some time by starting seeds in individual pots, as with melons. Follow the same fertilizing and watering schedule as for cucumbers and melons. Pick summer squashes continually, as you would cucumbers, for a steady supply of young fruit.

Time to sow seeds in place (can be started indoors 3-4 weeks earlier)

Zone/South		Zone/North		Zone/West	
1	1/1-3/31	5	4/15-6/30	6, 8, 13	5/15-6/15
2	1/15-3/31	6	4/20-6/15	9	5/20-7/5
3	3/1-4/15	7	5/1-6/15	10	6/1-6/30
4	3/15-4/15	8	5/15-6/15	12	5/15-6/15
5	4/1-5/15	9	5/20-7/5	14	3/1-4/30
6	5/15-6/30	10	6/1-6/30	15, 21	3/1-5/15
7	5/1-6/20	11	5/20-6/15	16, 17	5/15-6/15
13	5/15-6/15			18	5/15-6/15
				19	2/1-7/15
				20	5/1-5/31
				22	4/1-6/30

Spaghetti squash.

Harvest and use. Pick summer squashes when they are young and tender. The seeds should be undeveloped and the rind soft. Harvest zucchini and crookneck types when they are 1½ to 2 inches in diameter, and take bush scallops when they are 3 to 4 inches across.

Winter squashes must be thoroughly mature to have good quality. If picked immature, they will be watery and poor in flavor. The flavor usually is better

A sure sign of the autumn harvest—
a field of pumpkins ready for the
transformation into jack-o-lanterns.

after some cold weather has increased the sugar content. Learn to judge your varieties by color. Most green varieties get some brown or bronze, and butternut must lose all its green and turn to a distinct tan.

Don't worry when the first blossoms fail to set fruit. Some female flowers will bloom before there are male flowers for pollen, and will dry up or produce small fruits that abort and subsequently rot. This is a natural behavior, not a disease. The same thing happens when a good load of fruit is set and the plant is using all its resources to develop them. The aborting of young fruits is a self-pruning process.

Squash varieties. From a multiple list of 30 or more acceptable varieties, the following offer good representations of their class:

Winter squash: 'Waltham Butternut' (85 days): Good uniformity and production. Fine flavor. All-America Selection. 'Table King' (75 days): Bush acorn type. All-America Selection. 'Early Butternut' (85 days): All-America Selection. 'Gold Nugget' (85 days): Bush variety. Very early. 'Butternut' (95 days): Mild flavor. 'Buttercup' (100 days): Sweet, strong flavor. 'Table Queen' (85 days): Acorn type, early baking squash. 'Hubbard' (110 days): Large, good keeper. 'Banana' (110 days): Long, pink, grey. Jumbo strains available. 'Sweet Mama' (85 days): Heavy producer of dark grey-green fruit. Plant can be kept clipped to 4 feet.

Spaghetti Squash: This novel squash has the same strong vining growth habit as other winter squashes and is grown in the same way. Two plants will produce more fruits than a family can use.

The first fruits will be ripe in about 90 days from seeding. Do not pick until they are fully ripe—when the rind turns a deep yellow.

The flesh of the squash is made up of crisp, spaghettilike strands, which you can pull apart after the squash is cooked. An easy way to handle the squash is to bake it whole. Catalog sources are: (4), (14), (25), (26), (27).

Summer squash: Zucchini now comes in yellow, and in shades of green, gray, and black. Three of the hybrids are All America selections: 'Aristocrat' (50 days); 'Chefini' (48 days); and 'Greyzini' (50 days). Also on the zucchini recommended lists are 'Burpee Golden' (54 days); 'Burpee Hybrid' (50 days); and 'Ambassador Hybrid' (48 days).

Other popular summer squash: 'Early White Bush Scallop' (60 days). 'Patty Green Tint' (50 days). 'Scallopini' (50 days): Scalloped type, delicious raw or cooked. All-America Selection. 'St. Pat's Scallop' (50 days): All-America Selection. 'Golden Summer Crookneck' (53 days). 'Seneca Prolific' (51 days).

Pumpkin varieties. 'Cheyenne Bush' (75 days). Small early bush, for pie.
'Cinderella' (95 days). Bush, medium-size jack-o-lantern.
'Small Sugar' (New England Pie). (100 days).
'Jack-O-Lantern' (110 days). Medium size.
'Connecticut Field' (Big Tom). (120 days). Large jack-o-lantern type.
'Big Max' (120 days). Contest winner for size, not table quality.
'Spirit' (100 days). Compact vine for small gardens. All-America Selection.
'Triple Treat' (110 days). Hull-less edible seeds. Great for jack-o-lanterns and pies.
'Lady Godiva' (110 days). Hull-less edible seeds in a green and yellow striped pumpkin.

Serving ideas. The summer squashes—yellow crookneck, zucchini, and pattypan or scallop—play a role in most cuisines. They cook relatively swiftly, compared to the winter squash varieties.

Zucchini is excellent grated and steamed quickly in a little butter. Or slice it thinly and arrange the slices in overlapping rows in a large frying pan. Drizzle with olive oil and steam until crisp tender. Sprinkle with grated Parmesan cheese and slip the pan under the broiler until the cheese is crusty.

As an added bonus, you can enjoy the blossoms as well as the fruit. These

1. Cushaw-type pumpkins.
2. Squash, past its picking prime.
3. French pumpkin.

flowers are more than just ornamental—they are delicious when stuffed. You can use a prepared meat, crumb, or cheese stuffing.

Slice zucchini to cook in Oriental stir-fries or Italian frittatas. Split and stuff the squash with ground beef, crumbs, and cheese, and bake.

The yellow crookneck looks festive simply halved, steamed in butter, and dusted with nutmeg. The pattypan takes well to stuffing.

Winter squash are good to steam. Drizzle halves of hot, tender acorn or butternut squash with honey or brown sugar and butter. Or fill with browned sausage links. Children delight in steamed hubbard squash, mashed and topped with marshmallows, then baked until toasty.

South Americans favor pumpkin in soups, while Greeks bake it between fila layers for a honey-drenched dessert.

Serving ideas for spaghetti squash: Place the squash in a shallow baking pan and bake in a 350° oven for 1½ hours, turning once, or bake until the squash yields to gentle pressure. Then cut it horizontally and remove the seeds. With a fork, fluff up the strands. Mix with 3 tablespoons soft butter, ¾ cup shredded Parmesan cheese, and 6 to 8 slices crisp, cooked, diced bacon. Return the half shells to the 350° oven and heat 10 to 15 minutes longer, or until hot through. Makes about 4 servings.

Sweet Potato

Columbus brought this member of the morning glory family from Central and South America to Spain. After the conquest of Mexico, the Spaniards introduced sweet potatoes to the Philippines, where the Chinese learned of them. Portuguese ships carried these vegetables to Africa and Asia. Records show that sweet potatoes were cultivated in Virginia in 1648. No vegetable

More squash varieties:
1. 'Golden Nugget'.
2. Zucchini squash and blossom.
3. Crookneck.

Sweet potatoes.

Swiss chard.

commonly grown in the United States will withstand more summer heat, and very few require as much heat as the sweet potato.

How to grow. There are plenty of reasons why most gardeners should not grow sweet potatoes.

For one thing, sweet potatoes need space to grow in. The closest planting is 9 to 12 inches apart in rows 3 feet apart.

For another, they need a light sandy soil. When they're grown in heavy soils, the enlarged roots are apt to be long and stringy.

Too much water tends to make the roots more elongated and less blocky.

Fertilization is tricky. If given too much nitrogen, sweet potatoes develop more vines than roots. However, it's not a poor soil crop. Working a low-nitrogen fertilizer such as 5-10-10 into the soil at the rate of 4 pounds to 100 feet of row will improve the yield. Prepare the soil 2 weeks before planting.

If you do plant sweet potatoes, start them from slips. Plant small or medium-sized tubers close together in sand in hot beds. When the sprouts reach 9 to 12 inches (in 4 to 6 weeks), cut them off 2 inches above the roots and set them in a sterilized mix until the roots form.

You can buy transplants at garden centers in warm-summer areas.

Sweet potato in a box. If you would like just to sample sweet-potato growing, try growing one in a box or tub that's at least 12 inches deep and 15 inches wide. Use a light, porous soil mix. Place a 4-foot stake in the center to support the vine. Or grow it as a lush vining houseplant, indoors in a bowl or jar.

Varieties. 'Jersey Orange', 'Nugget', and 'Nemagold' are the popular dry-fleshed varieties. 'Centennial', 'Porto Rico', and 'Gold Rush' rate high in the list of moist-fleshed varieties.

Serving ideas. This delectable root plays a role in many cuisines. Include it on a Japanese tempura tray; it is excellent deep-fat fried. Dice it for a stew or purée it for a pudding.

Swiss Chard

Chard, popular long before Roman times, is a beet that produces edible leaves and stalks rather than edible roots.

You can harvest one planting over many months. You can cut the large, crinkly leaves and fleshy stalks from the plant as it grows.

The chard's greatest virtue is its ability to take the summer temperatures that make spinach and lettuce bolt to seed.

How to grow. It's easy and foolproof to grow. Sow the seeds in rows 18 to 24 inches apart, and thin to 4 to 8 inches. Use the thinnings for greens.

When to plant. Plant at the same time as beets. Since you can cut leaves from plants continuously, you won't need successive sowings. Even if you cut the entire plant an inch or two above the crown, new leaves still will be produced.

Varieties. 'Rhubarb Chard' (60 days). Dark green leaves and red stalks. A favorite vegetable for the flower border.

'Lucullus' (60 days). Light green leaves and broad white stalks. Mild spinach-like taste.

'Fordhook Giant' (60 days). Produces very broad (2½ inch), thick, white stalks and thick, crinkly, dark green leaves.

Serving ideas. Cut the thick stalks into 2- or 3-inch lengths and simmer in boiling salted water until tender. Serve hot with butter and a touch of wine vinegar. Chill and toss with a vinaigrette dressing.

Coarsely chop the leaves and cook quickly in just the water that clings to the leaves; dress with butter and salt. Serve hot cooked greens in a hot bacon and wine-vinegar dressing, and sprinkle with shredded hard-cooked egg. Or add coarsely chopped leaves to Italian minestrone.

Tomatoes

Of all the New World's vegetable gifts to the Old World, none took as long to be appreciated as the tomato.

Tomatoes were used for centuries in South America and Mexico, and were recorded as being cultivated in France, Spain, and Italy in 1544. But as much as a century later, the English grew them only as a curiosity. Seemingly, the first seeds to reach Europe were of the yellow variety, called "apples of gold" (pomi d'oro) in Italy, and "apples of love" (pommes d'amours) in France a few years later.

In pioneering America, only a few brave souls ventured to eat the fruit. New Englanders in Salem in 1802 wouldn't even taste it. But by 1835, *Maine Farmer* had recognized tomatoes as "a useful article of diet and should be found on everyman's table."

Good Transplant   Leggy Transplant

Time to set out plants (sow seed indoors 5-7 weeks earlier)

Zone/South		Zone/North		Zone/West	
1	1/1-3/31, 7/1-12/31	5	4/10-6/15	6, 8, 13	6/1-6/30
2	1/15-3/31, 8/15-9/30	6	5/1-6/15	9	6/1-6/30
3	3/1-4/30, 8/1-8/31	7	5/15-6/30	10	6/5-6/20
4	3/15-5/10, 7/1-7/30	8	5/20-6/30	12	—
5	5/1-6/30	9	6/1-6/30	14	1/1-3/31
6	5/15-6/15	10	6/5-6/30	15, 21	3/1-4/30
7	5/15-6/30	11	5/20-6/15	16, 17	—
13	6/1-6/30			18	4/1-6/30
				19	5/10-8/15
				20	5/10-6/30
				22	3/1-5/31

...Both should be planted deep. Roots will develop along the buried stem.

Starting from seed. Use the usual method of growing from seed, starting 5 to 7 weeks before time to set out plants. (See page 53; also see page 51 for directions on growing from seed without transplanting.)

Planting. When you grow or buy transplants, aim for the ideal—a stocky, bushy plant. Unlike other plants, tomatoes are set deep in the soil. Set them so that the first leaves are just above soil level. Plant leggy plants horizontally. (See sketch.) Roots will form along the buried stem.

Mistakes beginners make. Failing to fit the variety to the climate is one way to a disappointing crop.

Neglecting to choose disease-resistant varieties may or may not be a cause of failure—see page 61.

Planting too early in the season.

Trying to grow them in a shady location. The tomato requires at least 6 hours of direct sunlight.

Varieties. In cool-summer areas, select from the "early" varieties. Generally they will set fruit at lower temperatures than the late-maturing kinds, and they require less total heat. You may find special varieties selected for local conditions among the transplants sold at garden stores. 'San Francisco Fog' and 'Eureka Mist' are western examples. In the cool-summer areas of western Washington, the old variety 'Chatham' is recommended. Local climate adaptability may make some of the old varieties the best bets.

If you have had trouble with diseases, look for wilt-resistant varieties. Both fusarium and verticillium wilt live over from year to year in the soil, and can cause the vines to die. The plant will wilt even with good soil moisture. Verticillium wilt has many hosts, infecting eggplant, pepper, and other plants.

If your soil is infested, the only solution, other than sterilizing the soil, is to use resistant varieties. Where nematodes make it hard to grow tomatoes, look for varieties resistant to these root feeders.

The resistance of the varieties listed below is indicated by the initials (V), Verticillium; (F), Fusarium; and (N), Nematode.

The number of days indicate the approximate time from setting out transplants to harvest.

The words "determinate" and "indeterminate" (abbreviated as "Det." and "Ind.") indicate the growth habit of the variety. The determinates are the self-topping bush type, generally 3 feet tall or less. The indeterminates are the tall growers and are generally grown on stakes or a trellis.

Recommended varieties for the South. Although such standard varieties as 'Bonny Best', 'Earliana', 'Marglobe', 'Ponderosa' and 'Burpee Big Boy' are grown successfully where soil conditions are favorable and disease prevention is adequate, the gardener who has trouble with tomatoes should look for disease-resistant varieties.

'Atkinson'. Midseason (F.N.). Ind. Strong grower with good foliage cover with moderate resistance to early blight and gray leaf spot. Stake or trellis.

"Better Boy'. Midseason (V.F.N.). Ind. Stake or trellis.

'Burpee's Big Girl'. Midseason (V.F.). Ind. Good foliage cover. Large, meaty, scarlet fruit. Stake or trellis. 'Big Boy' with disease resistance.

'Floradel'. Midseason (F). Ind. Large leaves, good foliage cover with resistance to gray leaf spot and gray leafmold: sets well at low temperatures. Large fruit. Train on trellis or stake.

'Homestead 24'. Midseason (F). Det. Bush type. Good foliage cover.

'Manalucie'. Midseason (F). Ind. Strong grower with large fruit. Good foliage cover with resistance to gray leaf spot and gray leafmold. Stake or trellis.

'Manapal'. Midseason (F). Ind. Large leaves with heavy cover with resistance to gray leaf spot and gray leafmold. Stake or trellis.

'Marion'. Midseason (F). Ind. Good foliage cover with resistance to gray leaf spot and gray leafmold. Stake or trellis.

'Porter'. Midseason. Large vine, good foliage cover. Ind. Medium, pink fruit. Stake or trellis. Consistent producer in Texas.

'Walter'. Midseason. Det. Compact vine, good foliage cover. Resistant to gray leaf spot. Medium, red fruit. Ground or stake.

'Red Cherry', 'Yellow Pear' and 'Yellow Plum'. These small-fruited varieties are in a class by themselves. All are vigorous, tall, viney growers producing abundant crops where standard tomatoes fail. Can be grown as a hanging basket to drape down 3 feet or more.

Yellow or Golden. 'Jubilee' (72 days). Ind. Medium-large fruit.

'Golden Boy' (75 days). Ind. Large fruit.

'Sunray' (75 days). (F.) Ind. Medium-large fruit.

Paste. 'Chico' (75 days). (F.) Det.

'Roma' (76-80 days). (VF.) Det.

Recommended varieties for the North/Northeast. *Red-Early.* 'Springset'. (H.V.F.) 65 days. Open-growing Det. High yield of medium sized fruit. Concentrated set.

'Spring Giant'. (H.V.F.) 65 days. Vigorous Det. 1969 All American. Good yield of 1½ pound fruits if you're lucky.

Red Main Season. 'Moreton Hybrid'. 70 days. Large fruit. Ind. Stake or train.

'Fantastic'. (H.) 70 days. Medium to large fruit. Ind. Stake or train.

'Jetstar'. (H.V.F.) 72 days. Medium fruit. Ind. Stake or train.

'Better Boy'. (H.V.F.N.) 72 days. Medium to large fruit. Ind. Stake or train.

'Cardinal'. (H.) 74 days. Large, crack-resistant fruit. Vigorous Ind. growth. Stake or trellis.

'Glamour'. 77 days. Medium to large. Crack-free, meaty, fruit of mild flavor. Ind. Stake.

'Campbell 1327'. (V.F.) 69 days. Vigorous semi-Det. Extra large fruit.

'Heinz 1350'. (V.F.) 75 days. Compact semi-Det. Heavy yielder.

Red Late. 'Supersonic'. (H.V.F.) 79 days. Large fruit. Strong-growing, large, Ind. vine. Stake.

'Big Boy'. (H.) 80 days. Strong grower; heavy producer of 1 to 2-pound fruits. Stake.

'Ramapo'. (H.V.F.) 85 days. Strong-growing Ind. Stake. Large fruit.

Orange. Generally the non-red fruit are considered to be less acid but this is not always true. Vitamin C content of these varieties is not significantly different from standard reds. All about 75 days to maturity.

'Caro-Red'. Round, medium fruit; has 10 times the provitamin A of the standard red varieties.

'Jubilee', (72 days) and 'Sunray', (72 days) and 'Golden Boy', (65 days). Large fruit; has lower (1/3) provitamin A than standard red varieties.

Recommended varieties for the West. *Red early.* 'Early Girl Hybrid' (45-54 days to maturity). Ind. Tall grower. Uniform 1- to 5-ounce fruit produced throughout the season. Mild flavor.

'New Yorker' (64 days to maturity). (V.) Det. Compact plant. Medium-sized fruit. Mild flavor.

'Spring Giant' (65 days). (VF.) Det. Vigorous grower with large fruit. Widely adapted. All-America winner.

'Springset' (67 days). (VF.) Det. Open growth habit. Highest yield in Oregon trials.

'Willamette' (67 days). Det. Low grower. Crack resistant. Firm flesh. A special for cool-summer areas of Oregon and Washington.

'Big Early' (62 days). Large fruit. Produces over a long season.

'Sweet 100' (70 days). Produces an abundance of very sweet cherry tomatoes in unusual fingerlike clusters. Vigorous vine.

'Early Cascade' (68 days). A vigorous vine with an abundance of medium-sized fruit in clusters.

Red main season. 'Better Boy' (72 days). (VFN.) Ind. Vigorous tall grower. Heavy producer of large fruits.

'Burpee's VF Tomato Hybrid' (72 days). (VF.) Ind.

'Heinz 1350' (75 days). (VF.) Det. Compact.

'Floramerica' (75 days). Widely adapted and excellent disease resistance. Good foliage cover. Heavy production of uniform, round fruit. All-America Selection.

'Big Girl' (78 days). Large juicy fruit, resistant to splitting.

'Bragger' (75 days). Large beefsteak type with good resistance to splitting.

Red late. 'Early Pak 7' (81 days). Det. Vigorous. Stake. Arizona and California recommendations.

'Ace 55' (88 days). (VF.) Det. Widely adapted where summers are warm—eastern Washington, Arizona, California.

'Pearson Improved' (90 days). (VF.) Det. California-Arizona.

Yellow or golden. 'Jubilee' (72 days). Ind. Medium-large fruit, some crack resistance. Mild.

'Golden Boy' (75 days). Ind. Firm-fleshed large fruit of mild flavor.

'Sunray' (80 days). (F.) Ind. Called a "'Jubilee' with wilt resistance."

'Red Cherry', Yellow Pear', Yellow Plum'. These small-fruited varieties are in a class by themselves. Check your garden store for the 'Large Cherry' varieties. They produce the half-dollar-sized fruits you see in produce departments. Vine growth is the same as 'Red Cherry'.

Tomatoes in containers. Tomatoes adapt well to container growing, and there is a variety to fit every size container. Even the large growers will produce good crops when grown in as little as 2 gallons of "soil". Compensate for the restricted root space by applying fertilizers lightly but frequently. A special soil mix (see page 36) will pay extra dividends in healthier plants and improved harvests. Remember, as the plant grows, it will need more and more water and nutrients, on an increasingly regular basis. An attentive gardener must make up for the fact that the roots of the plant cannot go very far for what it needs.

In the last few years, a number of dwarf varieties have been introduced. These are proving to be more than novelties. The smallest is 'Tiny Tim', a 12-inch plant with cherry-sized fruits. Next in size is 'Small Fry', with 1-inch fruits by the hundreds—8 to 10 in a cluster. And 'ToyBoy', 12 to 14 inches tall, bears

'Patio' tomato.

'Pixie' tomato.

Tie to
stake with
figure-8
loops

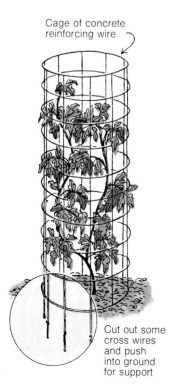

Cage of concrete
reinforcing wire

Cut out some
cross wires
and push
into ground
for support

ping-pong-ball-sized fruit. A new introduction is the 'Burpee Pixie Hybrid', growing 18 inches tall with clusters of 1¾-inch fruits. 'Stakeless' grows to 20 to 24 inches tall, with fruits 1½ to 2 inches. 'Tumblin' Tom' grows 20 to 24 inches tall, with fruits of 1½ to 2 inches. The 'Patio Hybrid' is a step larger, growing to a sturdy, compact 30 inches with top-quality 2-inch fruits. 'Presto' grows as a small-leaved, rather open vine to about 2 feet tall. It gives a heavy yield of half-dollar-sized fruits in 60 days.

Any tomato you can grow in a vegetable garden you also can grow in a container.

If you have unfavorable soil or potential soil diseases or nematodes, growing tomatoes in containers may be your way to success.

Your "soil" may be sawdust, wood chips, shavings, perlite, vermiculite, or any of the sterile planter mixes.

Your container may be a bushel basket, a 5-gallon can, a plastic bag, or any receptacle. Be sure to provide drainage, however. And if you use materials containing no fertilizer, follow the feeding methods of water culture or hydroponics. The material in the container must be kept moist. Water the plant with a nutrient solution (a diluted liquid fertilizer).

Staking-training. Keep tomato fruits out of contact with the soil to reduce damage from slugs, cracking, and decay. In wet fall areas, you can just about double the yield of usable tomatoes if you protect the fruit.

There are many ways to accomplish this. Every other gardener we have worked with has given us the "best way" to train tomatoes. Some of them are illustrated here, and more can be found on page 71.

Probably the favorite way to train large growing tomatoes is to make a circular cage from a 5-foot length of concrete reinforcing wire. The 6-inch mesh allows you to pick the tomatoes within the cage easily, and you don't have to prune.

Removing the suckers from a plant and training it to a single stake, as illustrated, is not the best way to train tomatoes for an all-season crop. If getting tomatoes a week or two early is that important to you, then single-stem pruning makes sense. But a 2- to 3- or a 2- to 4-stem plant will produce more tomatoes and with better foliage protection from sunburn than the single-stem plant.

The low-growing, bushy types are difficult to stake, but they can be held up by enclosures of fencing or frames of different kinds. You can let them sprawl; if you do, protect them with mulch or other organic material, or with black plastic.

Protection from the elements. Early planting calls for some kind of help to increase temperatures. If you use the wire cage, also use a cover of polyethylene film in the early stages of growth to boost temperatures.

You can cover a row of 4 or 5 plants with polyethylene film, as illustrated, and use it for early planting with a row tent only 2 feet high or for later protection against rain with a tent as high as the mature plant.

Failure to set fruit. The failure of a tomato plant to set fruit may be caused by several conditions.

The tomato sets fruit within a very narrow temperature range. You get maximum fruit set when *night* temperatures (at least for part of the night) are in the 60° to 70° range. Day temperature is not the controlling factor of tomato growth. If you set a plant out before there are a few hours of darkness with temperatures above 55°, the plant will just sit and sulk.

Generally, the early varieties will set fruit at lower *night* temperatures than midseason varieties will. However, rushing the season—setting plants out while the nights are still cold—is the most frequent cause of blossom drop in the spring.

In the summer, the high night temperatures (above 75°) will stop the setting of fruit. High daytime temperatures will also cause blossom drop.

1. Yellow Pear
2. 'Golden Boy' hybrid
3. Tomatillo husk tomato
4. 'Snowball'
5. Pear-shaped 'San Marzano' tomato
6. A big reward at the end
   of the growing season

Rain or prolonged humid conditions hamper fruit set. Growers in cool, humid situations have found that they can increase fruit set by shaking the plant, or vibrating it with a battery-powered electric toothbrush. If your plants are trained on stakes, you can hit the top of the stakes to release pollen, thus increasing pollination. The best time to shake the plants is in midday, when it's warm and the humidity is low. A plant hormone sold as "Blossom-set" can also ensure fruit set when used to spray early season flowers.

All vine and no fruit. The tomato plant may fail to change gears from the vegetative stage to the fruiting stage of growth. Too much nitrogen fertilizer and too much water in the first stage of growth is one cause of the failure; too much shade is another. You can help the plant switch over to the fruiting

'Large Cherry'

'Small Fry'

The small salad tomatoes range in size from the ½-inch 'Cherry' to the 1½-inch 'Large Cherry'. In addition to those shown here there are yellow cherries, red and yellow plums. 'Large Cherry' and the variety 'Basket Pak' are identical. All in this group, except 'Small Fry', rank as tall growers. The hybrid 'Small Fry' (VFN) with triple disease resistance is a strong-growing bush type.

Here the novel 'Orange Queen' stands in for several orange-yellow-golden varieties such as 'Jubilee', 'Sunray', and 'Golden Boy'. Fruits are low in acid and mild in flavor. Produces best in Northeast, Midwest and North-west climates.

'Red Cherry'

'Yellow Pear'

California variety 'Ace', smaller than average here, duplicates appearance and good taste of many main season varieties adapted to other climates and growing conditions.

stage by plucking out the terminal shoots, by withholding water to check growth, or even by root pruning. And whichever of these methods you choose, do follow the fertilizing schedule suggested here.

Fertilizing. Before planting, mix a fertilizer high in phosphorus into the soil. (See page 40.) This application will take care of the plant until the first fruits are set. Feed then and every month while the fruit is developing. Stop fertilizing when the tomatoes near mature size.

Blossom-end rot. The symptoms of this disease appear as a leathery scar or rot on the blossom end of fruits. It can occur at any stage of development. It usually is caused by sudden shortages or changes in moisture in the soil. Blossom-end rot is most serious when rapid-growing plants with high soil mois-

'Spring Giant'. An All-America selection with resistance to verticillium and fusarium wilt is well adapted to many climates. Gives heavy yield of fruits of excellent quality.

There are many Beefsteak tomatoes. They come in pink, yellow and red. This hybrid 'Beefmaster', formerly 'Beefeater', is as meaty as any and is resistant to verticillium and fusarium wilt and nematodes.

'Springset', a VF hybrid, is an extra-early variety with the ability to set blossoms in cool weather. Gives high yields where growing season is short.

The old-timer 'Rutgers' may be on its way out where plant diseases are prevalent but its virtues are carried on in new varieties in which it is one parent.

'Roma' represents the paste tomato varieties. It is very thick-walled and solid with few seeds. Widely adapted and excellent for canning whole.

ture hit a hot dry spell. Mulch plants with black plastic or organic material to reduce fluctuations in soil moisture and temperature. Do not plant in poorly drained soil.

Serving ideas. No cook needs to be told about the tomato's versatility, but a ripened-on-the-vine, garden-fresh tomato should be eaten as is, to savor its natural flavor.

Cherry tomatoes make fine appetizers. Cut them in half but not quite through, and stuff them with smoked oysters, small shrimp, or guacamole. Cherry tomatoes also are good sautéed quickly in butter and seasoned with basil.

Turnips And Rutabagas

Turnips originated in western Asia and around the Mediterranean in pre-historic times. Rutabagas are most recent, apparently originating in the Middle Ages from a cross of turnip and cabbage.

Though these two crops often are considered together, they have distinct differences. There are white and yellow forms of each, but most turnips are white-fleshed and most rutabagas are yellow-fleshed. Turnips have rough, hairy leaves, are fast growing, and get pithy in a short time. Rutabagas have smooth, waxy leaves, emerge and develop much more slowly, are more solid, and have a long storage life. Rutabaga roots are much higher in Vitamin A and higher in most other food components. The tops of both are outstanding sources of Vitamins A and C.

Climate and season. Both prefer cool seasons. Turnips do well in both spring and fall plantings, maturing in 60 days, or less. Spring seems to be preferred in the northern areas, but make the spring planting as early as possible. Not too early, however—too much exposure to 40° temperature will cause bolting. In warmer climates, fall and winter are preferred because the ripening period comes at the cool end of the season. The turnip's short season permits it to be grown, at some time, everywhere in the U.S. Rutabagas, taking 90 to over 100 days to mature, are grown only in the northern areas where summer average temperatures do not exceed 75°. Only one crop a year is possible; this should be planted to mature after the hot weather is over.

How to grow. The general soil and nutrient requirements are about the same as for beets, although these crops may need slightly less nitrogen. The seed bed need not be extremely fine because seedlings come quickly and easily and the enlarged roots are borne partly out of the ground.

Direct seed about ½ inch deep, in rows as close as 15 or 18 inches. Thin in stages to 1 to 2 inches apart, using the last thinnings for greens. Keep the crop well watered and fast growing, for best quality.

Harvest. You must use turnip roots before they get pithy, fibrous, and bitter. Usually they can be 2 inches in diameter; this varies, however—under ideal conditions they can be 3 or 4 inches thick and still mild and solid. Use turnip greens when they are young and tender as thinned plants, or grow special greens varieties such as 'Seven Top'. You can pull and cook these whole, or leave the plants for several harvests of the younger leaves.

Rutabagas usually are harvested after they are 3 or more inches thick. They have a long keeping quality and can be left in the ground after they reach usable size, or dug and stored in a cellar.

Varieties. The standard rutabaga variety, 'American Purple Top Yellow', matures in about 88 days. Some of the leading turnip varieties are:
'Purple Top White Globe' (58 days). Standard variety for roots.
'Just Right' (37 days). White hybrid for greens or roots.
'Seven Top'. Primarily for greens in late fall and early spring.
'Shogoin' (30 days). Primarily for greens. Will grow in hot weather better than other varieties.

Turnips.

Rutabagas.

Serving ideas. Boiled turnip greens are popular in the U.S. South, China, and Japan. The root is good sliced and served on a relish tray with dips. Or slice and boil it and finish off with butter; or mash and season it with dill weed or basil. Add it to soufflés or stews. It especially complements duck, goose, or lamb.

Serve thin slices of rutabaga raw with a dunking sauce. Or boil the vegetable and mash it to accompany goose, duck, or turkey. Dill weed and fennel complement it.

Watermelon

Watermelons require more summer heat than muskmelons do. However, in areas where muskmelons are grown, the icebox-sized watermelons are a better bet than the 25- and 30-pound varieties.

Time to sow seeds in place (for dates, see Melons, page 111).

Varieties. 'Charleston Gray' (85 days). Cylindrical with greenish-white rind. It is recommended frequently because of its resistance to fusarium wilt and anthracnose.

'Crimson Sweet' (85 days). The green-striped oval fruits weigh from 15 to 25 pounds. The flesh is firm and averages about 11 percent sugar. It is resistant to fusarium wilt and anthracnose.

'Kleckley Sweet Improved' (88 days). Long, dark green, to 30 pounds. Resistant to fusarium wilt.

'Golden Midget' (65 days). 6-inch fruit turns yellow when ripe.

'New Hampshire Midget' (70 days). 6 inch fruit.

'Sugar Baby' (75 days). 8-inch, dark green. Sweet.

'Red Lollipop' (70 days). 3-pound fruit.

'Yellow Lollipop' (70 days). Yellow flesh.

'Yellow Baby' (70 days). Small, icebox type. Juicy, sweet yellow flesh. Light green rind striped darker green. All-America Selection.

'Sweet Favorite' (80 days). Large, oblong fruit up to 20 pounds. Light green rind striped dark green. Sweet and juicy. All-America Selection.

'Sugar Doll' (70 days). Heavy producer of small (8 pound) icebox melons. Thin dark green rind. Sweet and delicious.

Several new seedless hybrids are becoming available. Look for names like 'Triple Sweet Seedless' and 'Super Sweet Seedless'.

Harvesting. Picking a watermelon when it's neither too green nor too ripe is not easy.

Some gardeners claim that you can tell the fruit is ripe when the little "pig's-tail" curl that's attached to the vine turns brown and dries up. The trouble with depending on this "sign" is that in some varieties the tendril dries up 7 to 10 days before the fruit is fully ripe.

The sound of a thump—a ringing sound when the fruit is green, or a dull or dead sound when the fruit is ripe—is not reliable, either—the dull/dead sound is also the sign of overripeness.

The surest way to tell if most varieties are ripe is to look at the color of the bottom surface. As the melon matures, the "ground spot" turns from a light straw-color to a richer yellow.

All fruits tend to lose the powdery or slick appearance of the top surface and take on a dull look when ripe.

Yardlong Bean or Asparagus Bean

Listed in catalogs as a heavy producer of 24-inch-long beans, this plant is actually a tall-growing variety of cowpea. It is a vigorous climber and is trained on wire or trellis. Pick yardlong pods when they're young and use them as you would snap beans.

Zucchini—see Squash

Sources

Looking for a scarce or hard-to-find vegetable variety? Check the "parent" vegetable in the Encyclopedia section beginning on page 74. If the variety is hard-to-find, listed in only a few catalogs, it is followed by catalog numbers in parenthesis. These are the same as the numbers in parenthesis below—showing you which seed companies to write to for the catalog you want.

A word of caution: Seed companies and catalogs change from year to year. Varieties listed one year may be dropped the next as seed companies keep up with the more popular varieties. Be a catalog snooper: they're a source of continual surprise.

Allen Sterling & Lathrop (1)
191 U.S. Rt. #1
Falmouth, ME 04105
Straight-forward listing of varieties.

Meyer Seed Co. (3)
600 So. Caroline St.
Baltimore, MD 21231
Vegetables; 23 pages.

Burgess Seed & Plant Co. (4)
Box 2000, Galesburg, MI 49053
44 pages, 8½ x 11. Vegetables 26 pages. Special attention to varieties for northern states. Many unusual items.

W. Atlee Burpee Co. (5)
Warminster, PA 18974
*170 pages, 6 x 9.
Free.*

D. V. Burrell Seed Growers Co. (6)
Box 150
Rocky Ford, CO 81067
96 pages, 8½ x 4¼. Special emphasis on melons, peppers, tomatoes and varieties for California and the Southwest.

Comstock, Ferre & Co. (7)
Wethersfield, CT 06109
20 pages, 8½ x 11. Vegetables, 11 pages. 40 varieties of herbs. Founded 1820.

Jackson & Perkins (8)
Medford, OR 97501
12 big pages on vegetables in the 40-page catalog.

Farmer Seed & Nursery Co. (9)
Fairbault, MN 55021
82 pages, 8 x 10. Complete. Special attention to midget vegetables and early maturing varieties for northern tier of states.

Henry Field Seed and Nursery Co. (10)
407 Sycamore St.
Shenandoah, IA 51601
132 pages, 8½ x 11. A complete catalog.

DeGiorgi Co., Inc. (11)
P.O. Box 413, Council Bluffs, IA 51501
112 pages, 8½ x 11. Attention to the unusual. Established 1905. 35¢.

Gurney Seed & Nursery Co. (12)
1448 Page St.
Yankton, SD 57078
76 pages, 15 x 20. Emphasis on short-season North country varieties.

Joseph Harris Co. (13)
Moreton Farm, Rochester, NY 14624
92 pages, 8½ x 11. Vegetables, 39 pages.

Charles C. Hart Seed Co. (14)
Box 169, Wethersfield, CT 06109
Vegetables, herbs and flowers, 24 pages.

H. G. Hastings Co. (15)
Box 4274, Atlanta, GA 30302
64 pages, 8½ x 11. Complete southern garden guide.

J. W. Jung Seed Co. (16)
Station 8, Randolph, WI 53956
60 pages, 9 x 12. Vegetables, 18 pages.

Earl May Seed & Nursery Co. (18)
Shenandoah, IA 51601
Complete catalog. 80 pages, 9½ x 12½. Wide choice of varieties.

Nichols Garden Nursery (19)
1190 Pacific TH Highway
Albany, OR 97321
88 pages, 8½ x 11. The unusual and rare in vegetables and herbs.

L. L. Olds Seed Co. (20)
2901 Packers Ave.
Box 7790, Madison, WI 53707
80 pages, 8 x 10.

Geo. W. Park Seed Co., Inc. (21)
Greenwood, SC 29646
122 pages, 8¼ x 11¼.

Reuter Seed Co., Inc. (22)
Box 19255, New Orleans, LA 70179
32 pages, 8 x 10. Vegetables, 16 pages.

Seedway (23)
Hall, NY 14463
36 pages, 8½ x 11. Vegetables, 19 pages. Informative, straightforward presentation.

Roswell Seed Co. (24)
Box 725, Roswell, NM 88201
29 pages, 6 x 9. Vegetables, 12 pages. Special attention to varieties suited to Southwest. Established 1900.

J. L. Hudson (25)
P. O. Box 1058, Redwood City, CA 94604
112 pages, 5½ x 9. Vegetables, 16 pages. Ask for vegetable catalog—it's free. General catalog, 50¢. Accent on the unusual. Wide selection of herbs.

R. H. Shumway-Seedsman (26)
628 Cedar St., Rockford, IL 61101
86 pages, 10 x 13. Complete. Founded 1870.

Stokes Seeds (27)
Box 548 Main Post Office
Buffalo, NY 14240
Also: St. Catherine's, Ontario, Canada.
158 pages, 500 different vegetable and 800 different flower varieties. Emphasis on short-season strains.

Otis S. Twilley Seed Co. (28)
P. O. Box 65, Trevose, PA 19047
64 pages, 8½ x 11. Special attention to Experiment Station releases, and disease resistant varieties.

Glecklers Seedmen (31)
Metamora, OH 43540
4 pages, 8½ x 14. Listings, brief descriptions of unusual, strange vegetables.

Geo. Tait & Sons, Inc. (32)
900 Tidewater Dr., Norfolk, VA 23504
Vegetables, 24 of 58 pages. Special varieties and planting information for eastern Virginia and North Carolina.

Vesey's Seeds Ltd. (33)
York — P. E. Island, Canada.
Features early vegetable varieties.

C. A. Cruickshank Ltd. (34)
1015 Mount Pleasant Rd.
Toronto 12, Ontario, Canada.
An 80-page "garden guild" general catalog.

W. H. Perron & Co. (36)
515 Labelle Blvd.
City of Lavalla, P.Q., Canada. H7V 2T3
Complete general catalog of 106 pages.

T & T Seeds, Ltd. (38)
120 Lombard Ave.
Winnipeg
Manitoba R3B OW3 Canada.
48 pages, 6 x 8. Condensed general catalog for Midwest/North region. 25¢.

Laval Seeds, Inc. (40)
3505 Boul. St.-Martin
Villa De Laval
Quebec, Canada
152-page general catalog. (Printed in French only.)

A. E. McKenzie Co. Ltd., Seedsmen (41)
P. O. Box 1060
Brandon
Manitoba, Canada R7A 6E1

Alberta Nurseries and Seeds, Ltd. (42)
Box 29
Bowden
Alberta, Canada, TOM OKO
48 pages, 7 x 10. Vegetables, 14 pages. Special attention to hardiness—short season.

Agway, Inc. (43)
Box 1333, Syracuse, NY 13201
56 pages, 8½ x 11. Thoughtfully prepared for northeastern states.

Johnny's Selected Seeds (44)
Albion, ME 04910
28 pages, 5½ x 8½. Many hard to find seeds. 25¢.

Kitazawa Seed Co. (45)
356 W. Taylor St.
San Jose, CA 95110
One-sheet listing of Oriental vegetables.

J. A. Demonchaux Co. (46)
225 Jackson, Topeka, KS 66603
Gourmet garden seeds from France.

Grace's Gardens (47)
100 Autumn Lane
Hackettstown, NJ 07840
16 page catalog of unusual seeds. Cost: 25¢.

Tsang & Ma International (48)
1556 Laurel St.
San Carlos, CA 94070
One page leaflet; 16 types of Chinese vegetables, including bitter melon and Chinese okra. $2 minimum order.

Bagna Cauda. From the Piedmont area of Italy comes this renowned hot dip for cold vegetables. (The words Bagna Cauda stand for "hot bath.") There the most popular dipping vegetable is the cardoon. Use a wide assortment of relish-style raw vegetables. The slender bread sticks, called *grissini,* are a choice accompaniment, also.

1½ cups heavy cream
2 tablespoons butter
2 cloves garlic, minced
6 anchovy fillets, finely chopped
  Assorted vegetables: cardoon, celery, fennel, red and green peppers, zucchini, cauliflower, mushrooms, cherry tomatoes, Romaine leaves

Pour cream into a heavy saucepan, bring to a boil, and let simmer, watching carefully and stirring occasionally, until reduced by half. Using a small serving pan, melt butter with garlic and anchovies. Stir in reduced cream and heat until blended. Serve over a candle warmer with washed, trimmed vegetables on a tray alongside. Makes about 1 cup sauce, or enough for 6 servings.

Index

Page numbers in italics indicate illustrations. Numbers in bold face indicate major emphasis. The Planting Chart for all vegetables is on pages 56-57.

Index

Page numbers in italics indicate illustrations. Numbers in bold face indicate major emphasis. The Planting Chart for all vegetables is on pages 56-57.